Treasure Quest: The Book

By Paul Hayes

BBC RADIO NORFOLK
95.1 FM | 104.4 FM | DAB | bbc.co.uk/norfolk

First published in October 2011 by Charity Goods, PO Box 695, Newport, South Wales, NP20 4ZU.

www.charitygoods.com

ISBN 978-0-9560777-1-4

BBC Radio Norfolk, The Forum, Millennium Plain, Norwich, NR2 1BH.

www.bbc.co.uk/norfolk

Phone-in number: 01603 617321
General enquiries: 01603 617411

General e-mails: norfolk@bbc.co.uk
Treasure Quest e-mails: treasurequest@bbc.co.uk

Treasure Quest is broadcast on Sunday mornings from 9am to 12 midday.

BBC Radio Norfolk is available throughout the county on 95.1, 95.6 or 104.4 FM; on 855 or 873 AM; on DAB digital radio; or online at bbc.co.uk/norfolk. Programmes such as *Treasure Quest* are also available to listen to for up to a week following transmission, via the website.

Contents

Foreword

By Peter Waters
Editor, *Eastern Daily Press*

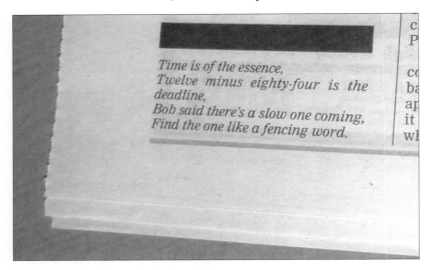

Time is of the essence,
Twelve minus eighty-four is the deadline,
Bob said there's a slow one coming,
Find the one like a fencing word.

There would have been a lot of readers of the *Eastern Daily Press* scratching their heads when they saw this odd four-line ditty tucked away in a dusty corner of the paper on Easter Monday in 2009. It wasn't a story – at least not one that stuck to the usual rules of saying 'Who? What? Where? When? Why?' By journalistic standards, it was gobbledygook. And nobody has ever said that about an *EDP* story! (We always worked very hard to make sense of Glenn Roeder's post-match analysis during his tenure at Carrow Road). Had the *EDP* finally relented and put a Poem of the Day in the paper? Nope, couldn't have been that – the lines don't even rhyme.

Of course, you know what it was. It was the very reason you're holding this tome in your hot little mitts – a *Treasure Quest* clue, a nugget of information for David Clayton, Becky Betts and their team of Sunday morning devotees to analyse and debate until they could see sense and send the BBC Radio Norfolk car off to the next destination, and possibly the fabled big prize.

Chocolate, I'm guessing, would be Becky's favourite prize, if not a book of 'Public Conveniences on the B roads of Norfolk' should she ever be inconvenienced, which is surprisingly often, if we're honest.

Waterworks aren't the only thing that can hold up the Questers... there are roadworks too, and tractors, potholes, pheasants, unexpected diversions, the last of which are most often caused by a flummoxed presenter back in the warmth and comfort of the BBC studio.

NORFOLK

Message led to hidden treasure

A cryptic message hidden in the pages of yesterday's EDP helped Radio Norfolk listeners take part in the station's latest Treasure Quest challenge.

The interactive show, broadcast each Sunday, was extended to Monday for a two-part Easter special. It allowed listeners to solve a series of clues and guide reporter Becky Betts around Norfolk under the guidance of show host David Clayton.

On Sunday night listeners were left with the clue: "Each one of these is something good/Directly slotting into the space/Putting seventeen under the new eleven/Paige to an old-fashioned knight/Ten steps from the edge."

The first letter of each sentence directed participants to EDP page 10 where they found the clue: "Time is of the essence/Twelve minus eighty-four is the deadline/Bob said there's a slow one coming/Find the one like a fencing word."

This led the team to the 10.36am train from Cantley to Norwich. The quest finished in Cromer.

The day after the Eastern Daily Press had teamed up with the Questmaster to hide a clue at the bottom of one of the pages of its Easter Monday edition, the paper reported on its role in the Treasure Quest two-parter.

The fact the programme endures is, I guess, because Radio 2 hasn't been the same since Pete Murray left Broadcasting House. I'm joking! The reason it endures is because it's compelling weekend listening; utterly riveting as erudite Clayton, dandy highwaywoman Betts, clued-up callers and a gallimaufry of genial passers-by attempt to unravel the devilishly difficult conundrums dreamt up by His Divine Trickiness, The Questmaster. It's what Sunday mornings were made for.

Oh, and by the way, the answer to the riddle was...

Peter Waters
August 2011

Award winner: Becky Betts proudly shows off the Creative East Award for Best Radio Programme, which Treasure Quest won in May 2009.

1

Treasure Quest –
The Story so Far

The story of *Treasure Quest* began back in late 2007, when a man called Martyn Weston arrived at BBC Radio Norfolk as its new Assistant Editor. He had all sorts of ideas for new and different programmes to try on the station, and one of those ideas was for *Treasure Quest*. Martyn was inspired both by a similar programme he had heard on the Luton-based BBC Three Counties Radio and by Channel 4's legendary 1980s TV series *Treasure Hunt*, which saw the inimitable Anneka Rice travelling by helicopter in search of clues against the clock.

Martyn Weston – BBC Radio Norfolk's Assistant Editor from 2007 to 2011. The man with a plan!

Martyn's idea met with the approval of his boss, BBC Radio Norfolk's Managing Editor David Clayton. In fact, Martyn not only persuaded David that the station should have a go at doing the programme, he also convinced him that there was only one man for the job of presenting it – David himself!

So on Good Friday, the 21st of March 2008, the team assembled for the first ever edition of *Treasure Quest* on BBC Radio Norfolk. As with all good programmes, it took time for the elements to settle into place, and it wasn't yet *quite* the programme you know today. David Clayton, Becky Betts and Navigator Ian Forster were all present and correct, but in the producer's chair with the honour of putting the first show together and masterminding proceedings was Amy Barratt. There were also two 'Treasure Questers' in the studio with David, similar to the old TV *Treasure Hunt*, with the idea being that the listeners would help these members of the public to guide Becky around the county.

The show was an immediate hit – when it became obvious that Becky had no chance of finding the treasure within the time allowed, there was such a deluge of protest from the audience that the following pre-recorded show was dropped, and *Treasure Quest* was allowed to go into a full fourth hour. Not something the Questmaster would ever allow today! What became of the *Quiet Gardens* documentary that was to have filled that hour is, alas, not known to history.

It was clear that Norfolk loved *Treasure Quest*, and a second programme was broadcast on the May Bank Holiday. There were still two members of the public in the studio, but behind the scenes the Questmaster and his glamorous assistant Alexajain Wills-Bradfield stepped into production duties for the first time, although Nanette Aldous had planned the route and set the clues. Graham Barnard deputised for an unwell David Clayton, as he would often do during the regular run; Graham also later became the first presenter of the companion show *Treasure Quest: Extra Time*.

Originally it was thought that *Treasure Quest* might be a regular Bank Holiday event, but by the time this second special was broadcast the decision had already been taken to have it as a weekly show throughout the summer of 2008. David Clayton was already presenting in the Sunday morning slot with a show called *The Norfolk Years*, and it was decided to rest that programme and replace it with *Treasure Quest* for a twelve-week run.

This supposed twelve weeks began on May 25th 2008. So far, we've gone well past twelve, well past a hundred, and there's no sign of stopping yet!

The Questmaster was already working on *The Norfolk Years* with David on Sunday mornings, and so inherited the job of putting *Treasure Quest* together each week and writing the cryptic clues for which he is now infamous. As the weeks and months and years have gone by, the programme and all those who help to make it have become increasingly ambitious. There have been clues printed in the *Eastern Daily Press*, and the *Radio Times*; two-part specials at Easter 2009, 2010 and 2011; encounters with the armed forces, police, fire brigade and all manner of lifeboats; journeys by train, steam car and vintage bus, and not one but *two* helicopter trips for Becky. There have been climbs up towers and descents into deep, dark cellars; horses to ride, sharks to

The stars of our show: Becky and David try to find a location on his famous laminated map of Norfolk, on stage for the programme's second Children in Need event, in November 2010.

feed and even the odd village sign or two! Plus, on one unforgettable morning on Valentine's Day 2010, Anneka Rice herself joined in the fun!

During its run, *Treasure Quest* has become the most listened-to programme on any radio station broadcasting in Norfolk on a Sunday morning. Rare is the week when the Questmaster is asking people if they will hide a clue somewhere in the county, and at least one of that week's clue-holders doesn't turn out to already be a fan. David Clayton is often heard to claim that, after a 30-year career encompassing not just BBC Radio Norfolk but *Look East*, Anglia Television and BBC Radio 4, he is better known for being Becky Betts's sidekick than he's ever been for anything else!

Becky confronted with a spiral staircase – one of her least favourite types of Treasure Quest obstacle! – at Langley Abbey in October 2010.

The *Eastern Daily Press* has hailed the show as "...a wonderful example of a local radio programme which includes – and relies on – the listeners' input," while *Norfolk* magazine described it as having "...built up a huge following [that has] reached cult proportions." *Treasure Quest* has also been recognised on the awards front, most notably when it won the Best Radio Programme category at the 2009 Creative East Awards, which celebrate achievement in television, radio, the internet and the printed media across the East of England. Later that same year, the programme took the Silver Award in the Interactivity category at the Frank Gillard Awards, the BBC's annual ceremony marking achievements by its local radio stations.

The programme's Facebook group has so far gained over nineteen hundred members, many of whom debate the clues each week. And there is little that demonstrates the popularity of the programme or the generosity of its listeners more than the thousands of pounds the show has raised every year for Children in Need. This has come from donations to comprise Becky's 'treasure' in Children in Need week, from the well-attended stage shows at the Norwich Playhouse, and from the 2011 *Treasure Quest* calendar.

Now this book is adding even more to the total we have managed to raise for charity over the past few years – so thank you very much for buying it, and for being such a fan of *Treasure Quest*. As Becky has often pointed out, we couldn't do it without you!

The Treasure Quest company, November 2010, pictured during rehearsals for that year's Treasure Quest Live! at the Norwich Playhouse. Left to right: Thordis Friðriksson, Kathryn Budd (Glams), Chris Bailey (stage show compère), Kirsten Thorne (substitute Treasure Quest 'runner'), Ian Forster, Becky Betts, Sophie Price (substitute 'runner'), Alexajain Wills-Bradfield (No. 1 Glam), David Clayton, Nanette Aldous (substitute 'runner') Jack Dearlove (stage show helper), Paul Hayes, Martyn Weston (stage show producer) and Bob Carter (stage show singer).

2

Becky Betts

Despite what some people seem to think, Becky Betts is a real name and not a stage name! Becky was born in Suffolk in 1978 and grew up in Haughley, near Stowmarket. As listeners to *Treasure Quest* will have gathered from frequent references down the years, she was educated at a convent school. Whether this left her pure in word and thought and deed, we shall leave it up to you to decide!

After she finished school, Becky followed her self-confessed "drama queen" ambitions by studying for a Performing Arts degree in Ipswich. It was during this period in the late 1990s that she made her first forays into broadcasting, working for Ipswich Community Radio and also joining BBC Radio Suffolk as a one-day-a-week volunteer on their Action Desk. The Action Desk not only dealt with queries from listeners about items that had been featured on programmes, it also organised social outreach projects, helping to involve the local community in various activities and campaigns.

Ready for another Quest, March 2009.

While being both a student and then a volunteer Becky held down a number of other jobs, including working as a barmaid, a cleaner, a factory worker and – so she claims – a bouncer! However, her talent for broadcasting was quickly recognised by BBC Radio Suffolk, and she worked her way into a full-time role there as a broadcast assistant – basically the name for the general dogsbodies who are the backbone of local radio. During her time at Radio Suffolk she also briefly

Scream if you want to go faster! Becky takes a ride on the scenic railway at Great Yarmouth Pleasure Beach, in April 2011.

worked at BBC Radio Norfolk, when she undertook a job swap. This must have given her a taste for life in Norfolk!

By 2003 Becky was working as a broadcast assistant on Nick Risby's programme. Nick is now known as the voice of late nights on BBC Radio Norfolk and the other BBC stations in the East of England, but at the time he was Radio Suffolk's mid-morning presenter. As a feature in his show Nick and his team often surprised listeners by making their dreams come true. The team decided to turn the tables by surprising Becky, helping her to get a taste of her acting dreams by having a day as an extra on the set of *Holby City*. You can still find the photos of Becky in a nurse's uniform on the BBC Suffolk website, if you look hard enough. Becky also began to be heard a bit more on-air around this time, featuring as a weekend co-presenter for Radio Suffolk.

It was in 2006 that Becky made the journey up the A140 permanently to come and live in Norwich, having got the job of running the Action Desk at BBC Radio Norfolk. In August of that year she gained a new member to her team when the man who would one day be the Questmaster started working for BBC Radio Norfolk as a volunteer on the Action Desk. Becky has clearly never quite got out of the habit of trying to boss him around!

Becky ran the Action Desk until 2008, when she changed roles to become responsible for the Big Screen in Norwich. This is a massive television screen located outside the Chapelfield shopping centre, a partnership between the BBC, Chapelfield, the local council and the London 2012 Olympics. With the screen, Becky is responsible for bringing all manner of national events, games and locally-made films to thousands of people every day.

It was also in 2008, of course, that Becky was chosen to be the 'runner' for BBC Radio Norfolk's first trial edition of *Treasure Quest*. It was the Assistant Editor, Martyn Weston, who decided that Becky's unique personality would be perfectly suited to the role, after she had already worked on several previous outside broadcast events for the station.

Becky was initially unsure about taking on the challenge, but – after she was persuaded! – she proved to be such an immediate hit in the role that there was no doubt she would be asked to do the full series. Her successful pairing with David saw the two of them given

Becky with one of her favourite treasures! November 2010.

their own Friday morning show from January 2010, bringing their *Treasure Quest* banter into the slightly more relaxed and controlled environment of the studio.

Becky's certainly had to go through a lot to earn the county's love and respect. She's battled through *Treasure Quest* in all weathers, and confronted her fear of helicopters (twice!). Through it all she has risen to become one of the best-known and most-loved voices on BBC Radio Norfolk, with her verve and gusto winning her a place in the county's collective heart.

Becky in fancy dress for a Children in Need Treasure Quest, November 2008.

Her enthusiastic "Hello!" – often heard on *Treasure Quest* as she rushes into each new location – was even made available as a download from the BBC Norfolk website in the early days of the programme, for people to use as the text message alert on their mobile phones. Becky once jumped out of her skin when she heard it coming from a complete stranger's mobile on a bus! And many's the time that a female BBC Radio Norfolk employee, when out and about on station duties, has been excitedly asked by a passing member of the public, "Are you that Becky Betts...?"

Perhaps Becky is best summed up by a description of her which appeared in a profile in the *Norwich Evening News* in June 2009: "She may not feel that she is like Anneka Rice, but her passion and energy for her job, and her unquenchable enthusiasm for trying anything once, undoubtedly makes her Norfolk's action woman."

Becky Betts – in her own words

I have this recurring fear with *Treasure Quest*, which is that we'll be stuck at the first location for three hours because nobody wants to play along and call in to help us solve the clues. Luckily, quite the opposite

This show is going down the tubes! Child's play in Fakenham, December 2010.

happens. Every week, without fail, hundreds of people offer suggestions, and I'm so, so grateful to everyone who takes part.

To those of you who give clear, precise directions to our location (no, not you David!), to those of you who have welcomed me to use your toilet, offered us food and drinks, given us the biggest, warmest, friendliest waves and smiles every Sunday when you've seen us, to the anagram and clue solvers… Thank you. The programme would not work, and indeed wouldn't exist, without you.

I won't lie – every so often, only for a split second, I miss my Sunday morning lie-ins, a nice Sunday roast at lunchtime, a wild late night out on a Saturday, visits to a Sunday morning car boot sale. But when Navigator Ian and I have ten minutes to spare at the starting point before the programme begins at 9am, we'll be sipping Ian's delicious, hot, steaming coffee, we look across fields, sometimes out at the coastline, or among the hustle-bustle of Norfolk villages and we remember how lucky we are. We even say to each other frequently how lucky we are to be part of the Sunday morning programme. The places we get to see, the people we meet, the amazing things we learn about Norfolk… All this instead of being stuck in bed with a hangover and aching limbs from dancing like a teenager the night before? I wouldn't change it for the world.

Becky Betts

14

3
David Clayton

David Clayton was born in Marske-by-the-Sea in North Yorkshire in the early 1950s, although he moved to Gorleston with his family in 1963, so he is very nearly a fully-indoctrinated Norfolk local. It was while growing up as a child in this seaside town in the 1960s that he developed his fascination – some might say obsession – with the buses of the period, something which endures to this day and often gets a mention when he's presenting.

In the 1970s, David became a long-haired Status Quo fan and tried his hand at accountancy for a living, but it was not to last. The lure of show business called and David moved into representation, working as an agent for bands, comedians and various other performing acts. It was during this period that David also became involved in broadcasting for the first time, presenting programmes for hospital radio in Norwich.

David Clayton: BBC Radio Norfolk's top dog.

Disco Divas of a certain age, however, may remember David best for his near-legendary stint as the resident DJ at the Ocean Room in Gorleston, where he spun the wheels of steel from the mid-1970s through until 1983. (He has also mentioned this once or twice on air, but we think he got away with it...). There are many stories told about his Ocean Room residency – some of them true. As well as filling the floors with Bee Gees numbers and overseeing Monday night Teen Discos, David also found the time to help set-up a trade union for DJs. There is no record of whether he ever led them out on strike!

When the BBC were recruiting staff in the run-up to the launch of BBC Radio Norfolk in 1980, David was quick to put his name forward, and of course the Corporation immediately said... "No." However, he was allowed to come in and help out by making the tea, and in the grand old tradition of local radio he worked his way up from there.

David's ambitions were not limited to radio, however. Throughout 1982 he worked as an in-vision continuity man for Anglia Television, introducing the programmes and filling those awkward gaps that might sometimes occur when said programmes failed to appear! David's duties at Anglia also occasionally included having to give what might best be described as a 'helping hand' to the station's children's birthday puppet, BC!

The following year David jumped televisual ships when he moved to BBC East, having to set his alarm clock early when he became the regular presenter of the *Look East* bulletins in breakfast television. Throughout the next few years he was also frequently seen on other regional programmes produced from the BBC studios in Norwich,

David in his younger days: a promotional picture for his Look East TV duties in the 1980s.

such as *Weekend* and *East on Two*, and was involved in presenting BBC East's inserts into the annual Children in Need telethon.

By 1983, David was also a regular presence on-air across the road from BBC Television, at the studios of BBC Radio Norfolk. That year, he became the co-presenter – with Neil Walker – of the show that perhaps really made his name in local radio, *The Norfolk Airline*, the station's new mid-morning programme. All of human life was present here, and it says something about the scope of its ambition – or perhaps the awkwardness of its presenters! – that to cope with the size of the thing, a wall had to be knocked down to increase the space in one of the studios, especially for this one show.

There was even a tie-in book published, *The Norfolk Airline A-Z*, co-written by David. Dog-eared copies of this tome can still be found lurking around the BBC Radio Norfolk offices to this day. In 1986 the programme won a Sony Award, the radio equivalent of an Oscar, and off the back of this success David and Neil were snapped up by national radio, working on programmes for BBC Radio 4.

David worked for Radio 4 from 1987 until 1991, and whenever an unusual or bizarre subject comes up on *Treasure Quest*, it's not long before he can be heard to say "Do you know, I once made a documentary about that for Radio 4...?" His series such as *The Local Network* and *Today's the Day* were praised by *The Guardian* newspaper, which in one review lauded David's "ebullient talents."

Once Radio 4 had finished with him David returned to BBC Radio Norfolk, where he became the Assistant Editor. In 1998 he was promoted to Managing Editor and he has been in charge ever since, becoming the longest-serving boss in the station's history. He has seen BBC Radio Norfolk through some of its most successful periods, with some of the largest audiences of any BBC Local Radio station in the country.

David has always remained a showman and a presenter at heart, however, continuing to broadcast in whatever slots his increased responsibilities as Editor would allow. By the mid-2000s he was fronting *The Norfolk Years* on Sunday mornings, and when this made way for *Treasure Quest* in May 2008 we like to feel that he had finally reached the very peak of his career!

David Clayton working the controls of Studio 1 at BBC Radio Norfolk, from where Treasure Quest is usually broadcast, in July 2011.

David Clayton – in his own words

The most amazing thing about *Treasure Quest* is that I now know so much more about Norfolk than ever I did before – and this from a man who has been on the local radio airwaves for over thirty years, a job where you can't fail to absorb masses of fascinating and trivial information about the county. I suppose finding out new things about the local area is part of the appeal of *Treasure Quest*, along with the amazing – she's not paying me! – Becky Betts.

I am stopped more in pubs, restaurants and on the streets of Norfolk and asked about this show than ever I have been in my three decades on the radio for anything else I've done. I've plied my trade on network radio and on television but it is for inconsistent map reading that I will almost certainly be remembered. I really don't mind. I can read maps, of course I can. I passed my O-Level geography with flying colours and maps hold no fears. I don't subscribe to the theory a SatNav is better and I don't own one. Having driven the length and breadth of the country for years as a radio reporter I sort of know roughly where all the major places are in relation to each other.

So how come confusion can reign during a fraught *TQ* programme? Well it's simple. I can't give accurate directions if the people receiving them haven't quite worked out a) where they are, or b) which direction they're facing. You see my problem? Then there are helpful 'local' directions offered by people at the clue location which can sometimes contradict those just phoned-in. Then my laminated map can fall on the floor… I know there is a place called Thornage, for example, but can't quite remember in which part of Norfolk it is hiding. All this under the pressure of the clock ticking away and Becky harrumphing at me. It's a thankless task, but someone's got to do it.

I suppose it doesn't really matter – it's all about the fun of the chase. Becky is one of the few women who can make me laugh out loud and I do sometimes 'lose it' on air, as you've probably heard. She's genuinely fun and funny and innocently outrageous; a contradiction, I grant you, but – uniquely in Becky's case – utterly, utterly true.

I'm happy to confess I have the easy bit, especially when the winter winds blow, but Becky and Navigator Ian are really lucky on those rare, beautiful clear days when Norfolk's countryside is basking in glorious sunshine on a Sunday morning. I wish we had a TV link rather than a radio one.

People worry that we all get a bit intense at times and might even detect a mild grumpiness at each other's shortcomings. In reality we like each other a lot and any tetchiness is generally directed at our collective inability to solve a clue or beat the clock. Anyway, let's blame the Questmaster!

So thank you *TQ*-ers for making us one of the most popular BBC Radio Norfolk programmes, and more importantly thanks for solving the clues. You'll have noticed I generally have little idea of what they mean and anyway, I'm busy man-handling my laminated map – that's my excuse!

David Clayton

4

Ian Forster

Best known by his *Treasure Quest* title of 'Navigator Ian', Mr Forster has been behind the wheel of the BBC Radio Norfolk radio car – and occasionally other station vehicles when the radio car breaks down! – since the original *Treasure Quest* pilot programme back in March 2008. He did, however, take most of the summer off in 2010 for other BBC duties, but for the bulk of the episodes during the show's run he has been Becky's careful and reassuring sidekick.

Ian on Treasure Quest duty in February 2011.

Before he joined BBC Radio Norfolk, Ian worked with the Norfolk Wildlife Trust, and listeners will often have heard his expertise on nature and the countryside during the course of the programme. He has also built garden exhibits for the Chelsea Flower Show, achieving 'Best in Show' and gold medal accolades.

Ian has come to the rescue of *Treasure Quest* on numerous occasions, with his careful and skilful driving around the county's roads and wide knowledge of the map of Norfolk. He's even been on driving courses with special forces-trained instructors to help hone his talents, but it's not just a driving job – he also has to be able to cope with all the technical demands of broadcasting while on the move, making sure Becky can be heard. He has even had to step in on occasion and take over broadcasting when Becky is indisposed – usually because of a toilet break!

He's sacrificed a lot for the programme, not just in terms of his time and occasionally his dignity – at least one expensive mobile phone has been destroyed while on *Treasure Quest* duty. This happened at Wroxham Barns in August 2008, when he and Becky had made their way to the top of an inflatable slide looking for a clue that wasn't actually there. They came down the slide together, having carefully balanced the technical equipment in their laps so it wouldn't come to any harm in the puddle of rainwater at the bottom… But they had forgotten about the phone in Ian's pocket, which was completely written off!

Probably Ian's most dramatic contribution to the programme came when the treasure was placed at the top of the wind turbine at the EcoTech Centre in Swaffham in November 2009. It was the day after the first *Treasure Quest Live!* stage show, so the whole team was feeling a little worse for wear in any case, but earlier in the day Becky had fallen over and cut herself on some gravel while chasing a previous clue, so was feeling far from her best.

She tried her hardest, but couldn't even get halfway up the wind turbine before having to admit defeat and sit down. In one of *Treasure Quest*'s most exciting ever finishes, Ian took over the microphone and ran to the top, finding the treasure envelope on the turbine's viewing platform with just five seconds left on the countdown, before promptly collapsing into an incoherent, panting mess on the floor! It later

Hero of the hour: an exhausted Ian after grabbing the treasure with only seconds to spare, at the top of the EcoTech Centre wind turbine in Swaffham, November 2009.

Very dapper: Ian on stage with David Clayton at Treasure Quest Live! in 2009.

transpired that the EcoTech Centre usually expected a fit person to make it to the top in ten minutes, an average person in about fifteen and tour parties take closer to forty-five with a stop along the way – Ian had done it in approximately five minutes!

Another of Ian's duties, something of a tradition on the show now, is that he comes up with the "quirky facts" about his and Becky's starting point on each week's Quest, which Becky uses to tease the audience about their location at the beginning of every programme. He is also something of a health and safety expert, always keeping an eye out to ensure that the situations in which Becky finds herself – no matter how bizarre in terms of broadcasting and her reactions to them! – are safe, sane and secure.

In the early days of the programme Ian's "bollards", used to alert other vehicles to the presence of the parked-up radio car, became something of a running gag!

Very occasionally, when the Questmaster has something big planned, he has to let Ian in on the secret for safety or for technical reasons – so he was aware that Becky would be taking her helicopter flights, and he was also told that Anneka Rice would feature in some capacity. He wasn't told where, when or how exactly she would be taking part during the morning, and his own personal theory is that he was told because he is "a little older than Becky," and would recognise Anneka in case Becky didn't!

When not on *Treasure Quest* duties, Ian is something of an outside broadcast specialist for BBC Radio Norfolk, and can often be found fixing up aerials, running cables and writing risk assessments whenever any of the station's programmes go out and about on location. He has

One of the certificates given to those who completed the special Treasure Quest challenge Ian created for the 2011 Royal Norfolk Show. This one was earned by listener Neil Collins and his family, who put it proudly on display above their Treasure Quest calendar!

been particularly involved with the annual extravaganzas from the Royal Norfolk Show, where we broadcast live. For the 2011 Show he even came up with a special *Treasure Quest* challenge visitors to the BBC Radio Norfolk stand could undertake around the showground, and co-wrote the clues for this with the Questmaster himself!

Such is his expertise with live events that Ian is even sometimes loaned to other BBC Local Radio stations to help them out with theirs. He does also occasionally work *indoors* at BBC Radio Norfolk, deputising as the producer of Stephen Bumfrey's afternoon programme, and he assists with the organisation of Children in Need events during November.

Ian Forster – in his own words

People often ask me, so what is it like to work with Becky? Does she really always want to go to the toilet? Is she always eating? Does she never get the jokes? Well, all of the above really, and Becky is a great friend, we work together like brother and sister, knowing exactly what the other has to do. Every Quest is an adventure; where we will end

Such is the popularity of Treasure Quest that the team are occasionally treated as something akin to local celebrities! Here Ian, Becky and David switch on the Christmas lights at Kingfisher Park, Burgh Castle, in December 2008.

up, what we will be doing from place to place. Keeping the car broadcasting is always a challenge too; the driving is the easy part, with the help we get from everyone.

I suppose if I were to pick one moment from the years of *Treasure Quest*-ing, it would have to be the climb to the top of the wind turbine at full speed with seconds to go. Towers seem to feature a lot; the Questmaster seems to like them. However, the best thing has to be the reaction we get every week as we drive around in the radio car. Everyone is so kind with the honking of horns and waving from their houses, and clue holders often surprise us with some delicious food, if I can get some away from Becky!

There have been some very funny moments for me too, like falling over and skidding down a bank at Bewilderwood on-air, or splitting my trousers at the Dickleburgh Christmas Tree Festival. Not forgetting when the car's mast froze solid and I had to send for a friend with a bucket of hot water. A cold Becky is not a happy Becky!

So thank you for your amazing help, it is so true to say we couldn't do it without you. For me, Sunday without a *Treasure Quest* to complete just isn't Sunday. See you soon at a clue near you!

Ian Forster

24

5

The Questmaster's Guide to the Glams

Treasure Quest would be nothing without the team of people who make sure the programme runs smoothly every Sunday morning. That includes the on-air presenting talent; the people who are kind enough to put the clues in place; the listeners

A trio of Glams: AJ, Thordis and Kathryn at the Treasure Quest calendar signing in December 2010.

contributing their ideas and solutions... and, of course, the people who always know what the answers are and where the programme is supposed to be going – the Glams!

These are the dedicated individuals who work as the Questmaster's 'Glamorous Assistants', answering all of your phone calls and helping the Questmaster to decide which ones are put through on-air. The Questmaster started calling them this at the start of the show's run as an off-handed joke referring back to the glamorous assistants of TV magicians and game show hosts in the 1980s, but the name proved popular and stuck!

We get so many calls that sadly we can't put every single person through to speak to David and Becky, but without the Glams – as the Questmaster calls them for short – we'd hardly be able to speak to anybody at all, as we'd be swamped by all your suggestions!

So to celebrate these unsung stalwarts of the *Treasure Quest* world, the Questmaster has penned a few lines to tell us all about the people without whom your voices would not be heard on a Sunday morning...

Alexajain Wills-Bradfield

No. 1 Glam and my right-hand woman, AJ – as we call her for short, because frankly we need something short to call her with that great long name! – has been the cornerstone of the *Treasure Quest* team ever since the start of the regular run back in May 2008. Always bright and cheerful, she is a calming presence when things don't go according to plan and I am tearing my hair out over the technicals! She has asked me not to mention her penchant for dressing up in oversized foam mascot costumes, though, so I shan't.

AJ also comes up with interesting suggestions for clue locations and sometimes helps to check over the clues to ensure they make sense. Her most dramatic *Treasure Quest* moments, however, have come during our encounters with some of the members of the team from Channel 4's old *Treasure Hunt* TV show. She had to drive out on a rescue mission to collect a stranded Wincey Willis after a radio car breakdown in September 2009, and in February 2010 helped guide Anneka Rice as she raced up to the BBC studios at the climax of her appearance – resulting in a photograph of a running AJ, Becky and Anneka appearing in *Ariel*, the BBC's national in-house magazine!

Originally from Bacton and now a Norwich resident, AJ studied Media Production at the University of Lincoln. She started working for the BBC in 2007, initially as a volunteer with the BBC Voices project,

AJ helps Anneka and Becky race to the treasure in February 2010.

and is a dab hand behind a camera as well as behind a radio desk. She directed *The Story of a Clue* video for the second *Treasure Quest Live!* stage show in 2010, and has also shot material for the BBC's *Look East* television news programme. On Boxing Day 2010 she stood-in for me while I was away on my Christmas holiday, acting as the 'Questmistress' and making a very successful job of producing that day's programme.

When not working on *Treasure Quest*, AJ is very much the Renaissance Woman of the BBC in Norwich, turning her hand to a variety of duties. She helps to produce Stephen Bumfrey's Sunday programme on BBC Radio Norfolk, and for television frequently works for *Look East* in various capacities, including directing some of their shorter bulletins. She can also often be found working in the frighteningly technical nerve centre of BBC television in Norwich, known as 'The Hub'. She helps coordinate the local BBC Children in Need activities every November, is the Assistant Producer of the 2011 *Treasure Quest Live!* stage show, and if you pop into the BBC's offices at The Forum in Norwich you might even be lucky enough to meet her filling-in behind reception from time-to-time!

In short, AJ is a woman of many talents and *Treasure Quest* could not happen without her.

The Lauren of York

'Lauren Tyson' when not on *Treasure Quest*, Lauren joined the team in February 2011 when AJ took a few weeks off and Norwegian Kathryn was promoted to the No. 1 Glam slot. After that Lauren often popped back to stand-in on the phones, before succeeding Kathryn as No. 2 Glam in the summer of 2011. David Clayton is always very pleased when she's working on the show as she's from York – the clue's in the name! – and as a Yorkshire exile himself, her accent reminds him of his childhood home.

Lauren arrived at BBC Radio Norfolk during her time as an undergraduate at the University of East Anglia in Norwich. While studying there she also worked as a presenter for their student radio station, Livewire 1350AM. As well as working behind the scenes on *Treasure Quest*, Lauren is a producer and occasional co-presenter on *BBC Introducing*, BBC Radio Norfolk's Friday evening new music programme for up-and-coming local acts. This latter role has seen her

The Lauren of York in the 'ops room' at BBC Radio Norfolk, during a Treasure Quest broadcast in July 2011. The ops room – also called the 'centre studio' – is where the phone calls are answered and where the producer of a programme works when their show is on-air. The station's two studios sit behind glass on either side.

appear on BBC Radio 6Music, and also resulted in chart star Ed Sheeran performing a live concert in her house!

She loves the BBC, and Radio Norfolk in particular, so much that she even made the station the subject of her degree dissertation!

Norwegian Kathryn

Although better known to her friends and family as 'Katy Budd', and despite the fact that you wouldn't necessarily know it if you've phoned the show and spoken to her, we did call Kathryn 'Norwegian' for a good reason – she moved to Norway as a child, and speaks the language fluently. This bilingual ability was occasionally demonstrated on-air during *Treasure Quest*, when we received correspondence in Norwegian from online listeners in Stavanger, which Kathryn was required to translate! She also entertained the audience at the 2010

Treasure Quest Live! with her Norwegian skills – she spoke no English on stage in the entire show!

Studying for an English Literature degree at the University of East Anglia tempted her back to British shores, and she joined the *Treasure Quest* team as one of the Glams following a period of work experience at the BBC in November 2009. She stayed with us as No. 2 Glam right through until the summer of 2011, when she graduated from the UEA and sadly moved on to more glamorous pastures – well, Peterborough, anyway.

Occasionally missing from the programme due to looming essay deadlines, watery trips away with her beloved UEA Kayaking Society, or even visits home to Norway, Kathryn was often bamboozled by myself and AJ discussing and quoting a variety of British comedy shows that, because of her Norwegian upbringing, she had never seen. As well as answering the phones on *Treasure Quest*, Kathryn also cropped up on other BBC Radio Norfolk duties every now and then. She worked on Nick Conrad's morning phone-in, Stephen Bumfrey's afternoon show and the Saturday gardening programme during her time at the station.

Viking invasion: Thordis Fridriksson and Norwegian Kathryn show off their Nordic roots at the 2010 Treasure Quest stage show.

Thordis Fridriksson

Half-Norfolk and half-Icelandic, an intriguing mix if ever there was one, Thordis was one of our main Glams back in 2008, and since then has occasionally returned to the programme as a substitute Glam on the rare occasions when the regulars are unavailable. A graduate in music from Trinity College, Cambridge, Thordis was also an alto in their choir and performed with them all over the world, including a concert during the BBC's 2009 Proms season at the Royal Albert Hall in London.

Thordis is known both for her sweet tooth – during her stint as a Glam she often brought in various home-made treats to keep us going during the shows! – and for her irrepressible enthusiasm. Her most notable moment on the show came in July 2010, when she created history by making the leap to standing-in for Becky as the *Treasure Quest* 'runner', the first of the Glams ever to do so.

Thordis has worked on just about every BBC Radio Norfolk programme you can think of, including being the regular producer for Stephen Bumfrey on his weekday afternoon show, on which she has also been a Bank Holiday co-presenter. She is the regular stand-in presenter of the Saturday gardening programme; is the producer of David and Becky's Friday show; has produced and reported from countless outside broadcasts; and was in charge of the Radio Norfolk section of the BBC's mammoth *A History of the World* project in 2010. This latter effort included producing and narrating a series of documentaries and organising several live broadcasts from related locations. She spends so much time at BBC Radio Norfolk that I sometimes suspect she secretly actually lives at the station!

Rosanna Wynn-Williams, AJ and Thordis during rehearsals for the 2009 Treasure Quest Live! show at the Norwich Playhouse.

Rosanna Wynn-Williams

Rosanna was a Glam for several months in 2009 before she headed off on an epic journey around South America and Antarctica, which you will probably be able to read all about in a book some day. She then briefly returned to the UK before leaving these shores again to take up residence in Paris, but has now given up teaching English in France to come back and teach French in England. She therefore probably qualifies as one

Rosanna is amused by David and Becky's antics at the first Treasure Quest Live! in 2009.

of the most-travelled members of the *Treasure Quest* family!

Her top *Treasure Quest* moment came in the week AJ had to go and rescue the stranded Wincey Willis. Trying to keep the show going, we strapped a broadcasting pack to Rosanna and flung her out of the studio to go and retrieve a clue that was, by chance, hidden across the road from us. She was very much thrown in at the deep end for her first ever live outside broadcast, but she managed to find the clue!

Not forgetting...

Joshua Hyams, a media studies student who helped me and AJ on the phones during 2008 and 2009, and was completely unflappable in the face of any *Treasure Quest* mishaps. These days Joshua can be heard as a presenter on Future Radio, Norwich's community station. And also BBC Radio Norfolk personnel and volunteers **Sophie Price, Edd Smith, Kevin Newman, Harriet Morter, Jack Dearlove, Hannah Johnson, Luke Tuddenham, Mal Lawrence, Rob Sykes, Kennet Tanner** and **Isabelle Neill,** who have all stood-in and helped out down the years when the regular Glams have been unavailable. I salute you all!

6

The Substitutes

As with any radio programme, not all of the regular *Treasure Quest* team are always available to work on the show. This might be due to illness, holidays or because they are committed to other BBC duties that particular day. And let's face it, with all the running around the county she does, Becky certainly deserves a Sunday off every now and then!

Fortunately, BBC Radio Norfolk has a ready collection of substitutes who are willing and eager – or can be coerced! – to fill-in for Becky and the other members of the team. If there can be said to be a '*Treasure Quest* family' at the radio station, then these are its nieces, cousins and uncles; people we might not necessarily see every week, but who we're always very glad to have with us when they do come to visit.

Kirsteen with her daughter Chloe at the end of a special Mothering Sunday Treasure Quest in April 2011.

Kirsteen Thorne

Since 2009 Kirsteen has been the regular substitute for Becky, and has stood-in as *Treasure Quest*'s 'runner' on more occasions than anybody else. A Norfolk girl through-and-through, Kirsteen comes from the tiny village of Pedham. She studied at Notre Dame High School and the University of East Anglia in Norwich, before starting at BBC Radio Norfolk as the telephone answerer for David Clayton's *Early Night* show on Sunday evenings.

These days Kirsteen is the producer of Helen McDermott's programme, a role she took over in the summer of 2011. Before that, she was part of the behind-the-scenes team producing Chris Goreham's breakfast show every weekday morning, and could often be heard filing reports for the programme; she also frequently stood-in on radio car duties for them if Wally Webb was away. Over the years she has worked on just about every programme across the station's output, including filling-in as a presenter on the drive time and afternoon shows and in the Sunday dedications slot.

Kirsteen always approaches *Treasure Quest* with enthusiasm and gusto, and isn't afraid to stand up to David and give him what-for if she thinks he's wrong about something or dithering over a decision. Her banter with David has also made her the natural choice whenever cover is needed for Becky on her and David's Friday programme.

As part of her *Treasure Quest* adventures, Kirsteen has had to go dancing for a clue (twice!), ridden a bike across Norwich, had to overcome her fear of fish to find a clue under some fresh kippers, and has even plucked a clue envelope from Navigator Ian's trousers! (Don't ask!) However, without a doubt her top *Treasure Quest* moment came on Mothering Sunday in April 2011. Due to some skulduggery on the Questmaster's part the treasure was with Kirsteen's own mother on the village green at Pedham, and her husband and daughter were also there to greet her!

Nanette Aldous

After Kirsteen, Nanette is the next most-used substitute for Becky, and it's always dangerous for the Questmaster when she stands-in, as she brings a quick-thinking, sharply-honed intellect that probably comes from her usual job as a journalist on the news desk at BBC Radio Norfolk!

Nanette started out as a volunteer telephone answerer on David Clayton's *Norfolk*

Quackers! Nanette meets some keen Treasure Quest fans in November 2008.

Years show on Sunday mornings, before becoming a full-time broadcast assistant at the station in 2007. Another born-and-bred Norfolk girl, as well as chasing stories on the news desk and reading bulletins, Nanette can also sometimes be heard as a presenter, such as when she occasionally stands-in on BBC Radio Norfolk's drive time programme when Matthew Gudgin is absent. Previously she had her own regular programmes at the weekend, being the voice of *The Early Show* on Saturday mornings and *The Show Show* on Sunday afternoons in 2008 and 2009.

As Becky's stand-in on *Treasure Quest*, some of Nanette's most memorable moments include finding the treasure with mere seconds to spare on Potter Heigham bridge during her first ever Quest; taking part in some rugby training with the Lakenham Hewett girls' team; and having to clamber into a dry suit at Mundesley inshore lifeboat's open day to qualify for a treasure in February 2010.

Nanette's cleverness was also put to good use behind the scenes in the early days of *Treasure Quest*. Before the regular run of the show started, Nanette planned the route and wrote the clues for the second pilot programme on the May Bank Holiday of 2008, so she's experienced the process from both sides!

Sophie Price
Sophie joined BBC Radio Norfolk as a broadcast assistant working on the breakfast show in 2007, and after a stint as the drive time producer is now one of the journalists and newsreaders who keep the station's news bulletins going. She can also be heard reporting for the

Sophie Price on Treasure Quest duty in August 2010.

breakfast and drive time shows, and in 2010 won the Original Journalism category at the national Frank Gillard Awards for her documentary on teenage pregnancy in Norfolk.

Sophie has stood-in for Becky on three occasions, twice in 2008 and once in 2010, and all of her Quests have gone down to the wire, with one very close victory and two narrow failures. Her most memorable *Treasure Quest* moment came in her very first Quest, as she raced to try and find the treasure, which was linked in with the legend of the Pedlar of Swaffham. Sophie, not familiar with this particular Norfolk tale, asked "So this pedaller, he'll be in costume will he, on a bike?" She's never been allowed to live it down!

Sophie also helped out on the production side of *Treasure Quest* in its early days, answering phones on the original pilot programme.

Nicky Price

Nicky is not only the voice of all the news and sport bulletins in *Chris Goreham at Breakfast* on BBC Radio Norfolk, she is also the station's sports editor. Originally from Worcester, she arrived in Norfolk to study at the University of East Anglia in the late 1990s. She has stayed ever since, working at BBC Radio Norfolk for over a decade now.

During her time at the station Nicky has worked on most of its programmes, including a two-year stint as presenter of the drive time show. She has twice risen to the *Treasure Quest* challenge, once in 2008 and again in 2010, but sadly failed on both occasions.

However, she insists neither was her fault – on her first go, she was frantically searching the treasure location for a man who hadn't actually turned up! (The Questmaster insists that nobody had told him...) On her second go, she was close to the treasure but got snarled up in traffic on Great Yarmouth seafront.

Louise Priest takes time out from Treasure Quest to catch up with some close personal friends at the market place in Aylsham, in May 2010.

Louise Priest

Louise first worked at BBC Radio Norfolk in the 1980s, and since then has worked across a variety of roles in both radio and television for the BBC in Norwich. She has presented *Look East* on BBC One, and enjoyed a record stint as presenter of the BBC Radio Norfolk breakfast show from 1996 until 2002.

These days Louise can often be seen presenting the afternoon *Look East* bulletin, and she also works on the programme's planning desk, helping to decide what stories to cover each day. She still enjoys presenting on BBC Radio Norfolk whenever she gets the chance, and regularly deputises for Nick Conrad on the morning phone-in.

Her *Treasure Quest* chance came in May 2010, when she visited the RAF RADAR Museum at Neatishead, encountered a bizarre array of *Star Wars* characters in Aylsham market place, and got well and truly lost while trying to find the straw museum at Colby! She blames David Clayton's map-reading 'skills' for that particular little adventure, though!

Wincey Willis

Famous as the weather presenter for TVAM in the 1980s, Wincey was also one of the on-air team for Channel 4's *Treasure Hunt*, to which *Treasure Quest* owes more than a slight tip of the hat. Wincey had worked with other BBC Local Radio stations in the past, so in September 2009 BBC Radio Norfolk's Assistant Editor Martyn Weston was able to persuade

Star guest: Wincey Willis joined the team for a one-off appearance in September 2009.

her to fill-in for Becky Betts one week. David Clayton had no idea who the mystery guest presenter would be until the start of the programme, and both he and the audience seemed impressed – and fairly stunned – that Wincey was actually taking part!

Sadly, the dramatic day didn't end there. With Wincey well on the trail of the treasure the radio car broke down in Wroxham, and the Quest came to a grinding halt. However, Wincey claimed to have enjoyed the experience, and it remains one of the most memorable *Treasure Quest* episodes.

Jenny Kirk

A journalist and newsreader for BBC East television, Jenny can often be seen presenting *Look East* bulletins across the day, as well as reporting for the programme. She has also stood-in as a presenter across various programmes for BBC Radio Norfolk, and twice filled-in for Becky on *Treasure Quest* in 2009. During her Questing adventures she often found herself leaping out of the radio car into patches of stinging nettles, had to try her hand at African drumming, and found the treasure both times, giving her a 100% record.

Lucy Clark

Lucy was the regular stand-in for Becky during the early days of *Treasure Quest*, filling-in for three episodes of the programme during the summer of 2008. At the time Lucy worked on the BBC Radio Norfolk news desk, but she later headed off to the bright lights of London, where she now works for BBC Radio 5 Live. She left her mark on *Treasure Quest* history, though, providing one of the programme's first really classic moments as she squealed and squirmed her way through thrusting her hand into a bucket of maggots to pick out a clue at Brundall Angling Centre!

Helen McDermott

Familiar to many as a former presenter on Anglia Television, based in Norwich, Helen first joined BBC Radio Norfolk as a stand-in presenter in 2010, making several guest appearances on the morning programmes. In January 2011 she was given her own regular weekday show, and later that month

It was never like this on Anglia! Helen McDermott goes Questing, January 2011.

was well and truly inducted into the Radio Norfolk staff by being thrust into Sunday morning *Treasure Quest* duties due to Becky being unwell! She returned for a second go in September 2011, taking another win to give her a 100% record.

David Whiteley

Since 2010 David has been a regular stand-in for the other David, Clayton, taking to the controls at the studio end of *Treasure Quest* when the usual map-reader is away. David is best known to BBC Radio Norfolk listeners as the station's Saturday Breakfast presenter, a position he took over from Stewart White in

David Whiteley has stood-in for David Clayton on several occasions.

January 2010. He is also a familiar face to television viewers across the East of England, regularly deputising for Stewart as the presenter of *Look East* – where he can occasionally be seen co-presenting with his wife, TV presenter and reporter Amelia Reynolds!

However, probably his highest-profile role is as the presenter of BBC East's *Inside Out* documentary series, on which he also acts as a producer, helping to put the programme together. As well as linking between the show's items every week, David also fronts many of their reports and investigations himself.

David was initially wary of taking on the *Treasure Quest* challenge, as he felt that the show was "too complicated" for him to be able to understand! He quickly got the hang of it though, and is very proud of the fact that – so far! – he has a 100% success rate as presenter.

Wally Webb

Wally has worked for BBC Radio Norfolk ever since it first started in 1980. For many years now he's been the presenter of the early morning show, and once that's finished he leaves the studio to become the roving radio car reporter for the breakfast programme.

As a radio car expert, he's been the ideal choice to stand-in for Navigator Ian on various occasions through *Treasure Quest*'s run, and his detailed knowledge of the highways and byways of the county has always come in useful! Wally is the only person to have been both the navigator and the studio presenter of *Treasure Quest*, standing-in for David Clayton for one episode in January 2010. On that particular occasion the Quest ended in failure, and since then he's stuck to radio car duties when guesting on the programme!

Keith Greentree plays a little air bass while waiting for a Treasure Quest to start in August 2010.

Keith Greentree

Best known now as the presenter of the Saturday morning country music show *Rodeo Norfolk*, a role he inherited from the late, great Roy Waller, Keith has worked at BBC Radio Norfolk in various capacities for many a long year, either presenting or working behind the scenes on several different shows. He's been one of the regular stand-ins for Navigator Ian on radio car duties ever since *Treasure Quest* started. He claims that – to his frustration – whenever he's substituting as navigator the Questmaster deliberately avoids setting the clues around the Dereham area, which he knows best! Keith is also something of a drummer, and in the 1970s played in a country band called Wichita. For a time, the band's agent was none other than a certain Mr David Clayton!

Bob Carter

A freelance journalist who has worked for several radio stations, including national BBC networks, Bob has occasionally been heard on *Treasure Quest* as the stand-in news or sport reader when the usual incumbents of those roles are away. He also helped set a clue once,

Bob Carter – or 'Billy-Bob Carter', as David Clayton named him for the day! – performing at Treasure Quest Live! in November 2010.

making Kirsteen ride a bicycle before she could have the envelope, and he made an appearance at the 2010 *Treasure Quest Live!*, showing off his singing and guitar skills as he performed *The Ballad of the Treasure Quest Trail*, a song written for us by listener John Elliott. Bob finally got his chance as a full member of the *Treasure Quest* team when he stood-in for Ian as navigator one week in August 2011. There's a rumour he was so keen to do it that he took the radio car training specially!

And not forgetting...
Graham Barnard, the man in charge of all the weekend programmes at BBC Radio Norfolk, who has regularly stood-in for David in the *Treasure Quest* presenter's chair... **Mike Liggins**, one of the most popular *Look East* television reporters and a former *Sunday Breakfast* presenter on BBC Radio Norfolk, who deputised for David on a memorably chaotic show in June 2010... **David Wootton**, a stalwart behind the scenes at the station for many years, who has several times stood-in as radio car driver... **David Webster**, a BBC Radio Norfolk

producer and sometime presenter, who filled-in for Ian as navigator for a tiring three hours wearing a broadcasting pack strapped to his back when the clues were all located around the 2008 Police Gala Day at the Royal Norfolk Showground...

Thordis Fridriksson, as mentioned in the previous chapter, is the only Glam to have stood-in for Becky to date.

One small step for Glam: Thordis Fridriksson became the first of the Questmaster's assistants to stand-in for Becky, in July 2010.

And even the Questmaster needs a break every now and then. When he does take a Sunday off he still sets the Quest up and writes the clues, but he has very occasionally allowed other people to look after the show in the studio as the substitute Questmaster or Questmistress. As well as his glamorous assistant **Alexajain Wills-Bradfield**, these stand-ins have been station sound producer and current *Sunday Breakfast* presenter **Emma Philpotts** (in April 2009) and former broadcast assistant and now occasional Radio 4 announcer **Luke Tuddenham** (in December 2009).

7
Extra, Extra!

Since it started in the spring of 2008, *Treasure Quest* has grown to become a broadcasting phenomenon which has spread into other parts of the BBC Radio Norfolk schedule, onto other radio stations and even out of radio altogether into stage shows, a calendar and this very book which you now have in your hands.

It seems to have become so big that Sunday mornings aren't enough to hold it all in, which is why over the course of its life it has spawned two spin-off programmes on BBC Radio Norfolk.

Treasure Quest: Extra Time

As regular listeners will know, Becky quite often fails to find the treasure in time. Occasionally, if she's very close to the final location or it's a particularly interesting one, the Questmaster will allow her to go there anyway – and this sometimes means that *Treasure Quest* spills over into the following show.

In the early days of *Treasure Quest* this was the dedications programme, presented first by Andy Archer and then Stephen Bumfrey. Stephen in particular was always happy to dip back into *Treasure Quest* after the news at midday, to see whether Becky had managed to reach the final location. Then, when Nick Conrad took over the slot

Added extra: Nick Conrad presented the show after Treasure Quest in 2009 and 2010.

following *Treasure Quest* in September 2009, he seized upon the connection to the preceding show all the more enthusiastically, being something of a *Treasure Quest* fan.

Nick christened the first hour of his new show on Sundays 'Treasure Quest: Extra Time', and would pick up on some fact or incident that had occurred in the programme to base a phone-in around during that hour. For example, on the day Becky found a clue on one of the helicopters at Norfolk Model Helicopter Club, he decided to get people to confess their unusual – and expensive! – hobbies.

Helicopters of a larger kind also came into Nick's show, as when Becky went on her first helicopter flight for *Treasure Quest* in October 2009 the preparations and instructions needed meant that she didn't take off until after twelve. So it was in Nick's show that the grand event itself and Becky's subsequent happy reaction to it after landing were broadcast.

On occasion, Nick himself ended up becoming more involved with the parent programme. At Easter 2010, the climax to the first day of the two-parter was supposed to involve David having to leave the studio and go up to the roof of The Forum, the building in Norwich where BBC Radio Norfolk has been based since 2003, to retrieve a clue. However, David had hurt his back and was in no condition to go running after a clue, especially up so many flights of stairs, so Nick was sent out to find the envelope in his place.

In January 2011, Nick left the Sunday slot when his weekday morning phone-in show was extended from four to five days a week. In his place the 12 o'clock slot on a Sunday saw *Treasure Quest: Extra Time* being turned into a one-hour show in its own right, now presented by Graham Barnard. *Treasure Quest: Extra Time* was jokingly referred to by Graham as the "red button spin-off show" from the main programme, and as well as carrying on with the phone-in element relating to something that had come up during *Treasure Quest*, it saw Graham playing musical montages and clips of funny moments from the morning's Quest, finding out a bit more about some of the clue locations that had been visited by chatting on the phone with one or two of the day's clue-holders, and often catching up with a grumpy Becky after the news if she had just failed to find the treasure in time!

Treasure Quest: Extra Time was by no means Graham Barnard's first involvement with the Sunday morning adventures, however. He

Graham Barnard was the original presenter of Treasure Quest: Extra Time as a stand-alone show, before the Questmaster took over the programme in August 2011.

has been part of the *Treasure Quest* family right from the start, and has often been a stand-in for David Clayton at the studio end of the show. After a narrow escape from life as an estate agent, Graham started his career at BBC Radio Norfolk like so many others, coming in as a volunteer to answer phones. He gradually worked his way up to become a producer and then a presenter, having been the voice of breakfast, mid-morning, the afternoons and drive time at various points during his time with the station. He has even previously been in charge of BBC Radio Norfolk for a period, while David Clayton was seconded to duties elsewhere in the Corporation.

Since January 2010 Graham has been the station's weekend programmes editor, looking after all of the shows broadcast on Saturday, Sunday and – in true LWT fashion, much to his delight as an ITV history anorak! – a little bit of Friday as well. This not only made him the perfect person to present *Extra Time* as a stand-alone show, but it also means he is usually the person who checks and approves the Questmaster's plans and clues for each Sunday. But not if he's filling-in for David that week, of course!

Speaking of the Questmaster, he often stood-in as presenter of *Extra Time* if Graham Barnard was away or on other duties. In August 2011, with more editorial roles being added to Graham's plate, he handed over the reins of *Extra Time* to the Questmaster on a permanent basis, meaning the cryptic clue-writer now has his very own programme.

David and Becky have fun and games on Fridays as well as on Sundays.

David and Becky

Finding out more about clue locations and some of the people who have put them there for us isn't just confined to *Treasure Quest: Extra Time*. It's also one of the elements of David and Becky's Friday morning show, which has been broadcast since January 2010. Their banter on *Treasure Quest* had proved so popular that it was decided to give them their own show together in the studio once a week – and so far they have survived without the atmosphere becoming *too* fraught!

Every week they speak to a 'Quest Guest' – a past *Treasure Quest* clue-holder, or someone who is involved with one of the locations where we have been, who can talk in a bit more detail about the location or organisation than the wham-bam format of *Treasure Quest* usually allows. It's meant listeners have had the chance to hear some fascinating stories that there simply wasn't time to go into on *Treasure Quest*, and it makes amends for so often only being able to rush in and out without stopping to chat.

The David and Becky show on a Friday has also given the chance for other members of the *Treasure Quest* family to take to the microphone. Graham Barnard and David Whiteley have often stood-in for David Clayton as Becky's Friday sidekick, and even the Questmaster has had a go at presenting with her, as well as occasionally deputising as the show's producer. Since August 2011 the show has been produced by Thordis Fridriksson, one of the Questmaster's former Glams, and frequent *Treasure Quest* substitute Kirsteen Thorne regularly stands-in for Becky, giving the programme a true feeling of being part of the *Treasure Quest* universe.

Elsewhere on the radio

Since BBC Radio Norfolk launched *Treasure Quest*, various other BBC Local Radio stations across the country have seen the success of the programme and started their own similar shows – some of which are also called *Treasure Quest*! Stations in Manchester, Suffolk, Lincolnshire, Shropshire, Northampton and Essex have all broadcast their own takes on the format at various points, and more often than not they have come to BBC Radio Norfolk first, to see how it's done and learn how to put the programme together.

But Norfolk doesn't just share its expertise with other BBC Local Radio stations. We've also seen our own version of the programme, and particularly our star Becky Betts, turn up – albeit rather unexpectedly! – among the bright lights of network radio. This happened when Becky's legendary Easter Monday helicopter ride in 2010 was broadcast again the following day... on BBC Radio 1!

This was all because some listeners to Greg James's programme on Radio 1 happened to have heard Becky's flight, and her extraordinary reaction to it, while driving, and it made them laugh so much they recommended Greg play a clip in his 'Best Bit of the Radio From Yesterday' slot. Greg started his radio career in Norwich, broadcasting on and later running the University of East Anglia's Livewire 1350AM, and doing work experience at... you guessed it, BBC Radio Norfolk! So he happily took up the chance to play a clip from his old station, putting out a

National exposure: Becky's Easter 2010 helicopter trip brought Treasure Quest to the listeners of BBC Radio 1!

couple of minutes of edited highlights of Becky's helicopter adventure.

The clip proved so popular that he was inundated with requests to play it for a second time, and he repeated the excerpt in his end-of-year round-up in December 2010, as one of the 'Best Bits of the Radio From the Year', and then played it again in an August 2011 selection. National fame at last for Becky!

Treasure Quest's appearance on BBC Radio 1 featured as one of the clips used in a special documentary all about the history of the programme, broadcast on BBC Radio Norfolk on Bank Holiday Monday, the 3rd of January 2011. Called *The Story of Treasure Quest*, this 55-minute programme – made by the Questmaster himself, and narrated by Nick Conrad – saw all of the team interviewed, featured a host of classic and rare clips, explored how the show came into being, and gave an insight into what David and Becky really thought about some of its most famous moments.

An annual two-hour *Best of the Quest* compilation, showcasing the highlights of the year's *Treasure Quest* programmes, has also been a favourite in the BBC Radio Norfolk Christmas and New Year schedules since 2008.

Treasure Quest Live!

Treasure Quest's first brush with the BBC's annual Children in Need charity appeal came in November 2008. The week before Children in

Need, a listener called Cathy Pye e-mailed to suggest that the show solicit donations from the audience, and make the total figure donated in *Treasure Quest*'s name Becky's treasure the following Sunday.

David Clayton was immediately taken with the idea, thinking it might raise a few hundred pounds for the

Who's that? Navigator Ian blindfolds Becky for a game of 'Guess the Guest' during Treasure Quest Live! 2010.

charity. He and everyone else at BBC Radio Norfolk were staggered when the figure raised, in only one week, reached just under £4000 – as was Becky, who was reduced to tears when she opened the treasure envelope to discover the amount.

It was clear that *Treasure Quest*'s large and loyal audience could be harnessed as a force for good, so when the following year the BBC decided that its local radio stations should each adopt 'Put on a Show for Pudsey' as the theme of their Children in Need fundraising, *Treasure Quest* was the ideal vehicle for the BBC Radio Norfolk effort. David and Becky had already proved to be a big draw for live crowds when they made an appearance on the BBC Radio Norfolk stand at the Royal Norfolk Show in the summer of 2009.

So *Treasure Quest Live!* was born, with the event being held at the Norwich Playhouse on Saturday the 21st of November 2009. Tony Mallion and Nick Conrad compèred the matinee and evening performances, respectively, with both houses sold out. Highlights included Becky being surprised by a topless wrestler – whom she found rather pleasing to the touch – and an unexpected guest appearance

The dream team: David, Becky and some of the Glams and substitutes line up to sign calendars after Treasure Quest Live! in November 2010.

Sign here please! Ian, David and Becky meet some of their public at the calendar signing in the BBC Radio Norfolk reception, December 2010.

from her father; a special behind-the-scenes video; David Clayton finding himself having to take part in a *Generation Game*-style against-the-clock painting contest; and a map-folding competition with some members of the audience.

The event was a great success, and raised over £4500 for Children in Need, along with another £1500 of donations being submitted in *Treasure Quest*'s name that year. Almost immediately afterwards, the Norwich Playhouse was booked for the same weekend the following year, and *Treasure Quest Live – The Sequel!* duly followed on November 20th 2010. Chris Bailey and Nick Conrad took on matinee and evening compèring duties, and some of the funniest moments included Becky's encounter with a Dalek, the Glams having to mime place names such as 'Gay's Staithe' during a game of 'Give Us a Clue... Location', and Becky's karaoke rendition of *Jolene* at the finale! The show was recorded, and highlights were broadcast on Sunday 19th December 2010, a day when the snow was so bad that it was decided not to send Becky and Ian out in the radio car, but to keep them in the studio with

David instead, playing these live show clips and answering listener questions.

The second stage show raised thousands more pounds for Children in Need, but not just from ticket sales. People were also buying a piece of merchandise that had been produced to sell at the event – a special *Treasure Quest* 2011 calendar. Also available to buy online and in Norwich, the calendar proved another great success, and a signing session was held in the BBC Radio Norfolk reception in early December, at which even the Questmaster put in an appearance. This caused almost everyone who queued up to have their calendar signed to remark: "He's much younger than you'd expect, isn't he? We thought he'd be about fifty!" Or, as one woman put it, "Isn't he little?"

There is an opportunity to see the Questmaster, as well as David and the Glams, in the flesh every week, as *Treasure Quest* forms one of the most popular elements of the BBC Norwich studio tours which take place each Sunday. Members of the morning tour groups get to see the studio team at work on the show as it goes out live.

Becky, David and their close personal friend Pudsey promote the Treasure Quest 2011 calendar at the offices of BBC Radio Norfolk.

8

Anatomy of a Treasure Quest

For most people *Treasure Quest* is all about the time the programme is on-air, between nine and twelve on a Sunday morning. Even for Becky and Ian out in the radio car, it's only an hour or two more on either side of that, as they take the car to its starting point and then come back to the BBC Radio Norfolk studios afterwards.

However, before nine o'clock on a Sunday morning rolls around again, the route of the Quest needs to be planned and the clues need to be written. This, of course, is the job of the Questmaster. So we thought we would get him to give you a quick guide to what goes into putting *Treasure Quest* together each week.

Man of mystery: the Questmaster as he appeared on stage at the 2010 Treasure Quest Live! show.

Treasure Quest – Sunday 20th February 2011

Hello, the Questmaster here. I thought the easiest way to show you how *Treasure Quest* works would be to pick a random example from the programme's recent past and go through what went into it and why. I've picked the 20th of February 2011 because it was a fairly standard five-clue show, and because all of the regular team members were present and correct on that day.

Usually I start putting together the new Quest on the Monday after the previous show, although it's sometimes earlier than that because someone might have written to me suggesting a good clue location for a particular date. This was the case here, when I'd been contacted some weeks earlier by Anthea Foster, the Norfolk

County Organiser for the National Gardens Scheme, which arranges for private gardens to be opened up to the public to raise money for charity. Anthea's helped out with *Treasure Quest* many times in the past, suggesting several NGS open gardens which have ended up being clue locations.

For this particular Sunday she had suggested that the gardens at Bagthorpe Hall in West Norfolk, which were open for a snowdrop walk, would be a good place to hide a clue. I was very happy with this idea because we hadn't been to West Norfolk with the show for a few weeks, and I always like to try and rotate the programme around different parts of the county as often as possible, so that everyone gets a fair crack.

Anthea gave me the owner's contact details and they were happy to take part, suggesting that the clue be hidden at the old ice house on the grounds. Once Bagthorpe had been arranged as one of the locations, I remembered I had also been contacted by a lady suggesting that the ruins of the castle in her home village of Mileham would be a good clue location, and saying that she would be happy to arrange this.

Whenever anybody writes to me suggesting a clue location, I always make a note of it and the contact details for the person. That way, I have a list of possible future clue hiding places I can always consult when planning the programmes. As having a clue at Bagthorpe had placed this week's Quest in West Norfolk, Mileham seemed a good fit and when I contacted the lady concerned, she was available on this Sunday and happy to help out.

The distance was a bit too far between Mileham and Bagthorpe to go straight from one to the other – I like to keep the travelling distances down to at most twenty minutes – so I needed somewhere else as a location between them. Also, as I had agreed that they would get to Baghtorpe at around eleven o'clock, I needed another couple of places after that to finish off the Quest.

To work out travelling distances and possible locations, I normally use an online map and journey time calculator, where I can just punch in place names and it tells me the average driving times between them. There'd be no opportunity for me to go out and about on the roads of Norfolk and test out routes, as I have various other BBC duties during the week – and besides which, I can't drive!

After consulting the maps and looking back over my records of previous *Treasure Quest* episodes to see where we hadn't been before, or hadn't been for a while, I decided that Helhoughton, Hillington and South Wootton would be good locations to try and use for the remaining clues and the treasure. You may have noticed that *Treasure Quest* can vary between having four or five clues – this tends to depend on what I can set up in time, what the travelling distances between different locations are, and how easy or difficult I feel like making it for you in a particular week! Of course, for the annual Easter two-parters, we have had as many as ten or eleven clues.

Here I fell back on my tried-and-tested *Treasure Quest* tactic of calling the local parish council clerks to see whether there was somewhere in their villages that might make a good location for us to use, and whether there was anybody who might be willing to put a clue or treasure in place for us. This worked well, and all three villages ended up having somewhere for us to go and someone who would help us – *Treasure Quest* would soon fall apart if there weren't so many people ready and willing to give up their time for us on a Sunday morning!

Usually I like to have everything set up, at the very latest, by Thursday morning – I like to send the clues out in the post on Thursday afternoon so that they have a couple of days to arrive at their locations. Of course, sometimes this isn't possible – during periods of

Becky gets ready to start this particular Quest in Great Palgrave.

heavy snow or postal strikes I have had to e-mail the clues out, or even dictate them down the phone. And sometimes I plant clues that aren't written down and concealed in envelopes, such as when I hid a clue in a photo gallery on the BBC Norfolk website, or secreted one in the Helen McDermott programme so listeners had to go back and find it using the 'Listen Again' facility online.

This week they were all written-down and printed-out, as usual. I enjoy the clue writing process, and actually find it the easiest part of the show – far

Someone left Becky a little hint of which way to head at the castle ruins in Mileham!

simpler than sorting out all of the locations every week! The clues can contain all sorts of elements, be it anagrams, facts and folklore about the location, homophones, references to pop stars, songs, films or TV programmes... something for everyone across the morning, I like to feel!

Once the clues are written, before I send them out I always get a senior member of staff to check them to ensure they make sense when unravelled and that people won't feel cheated. These days this is usually done by our weekend editor, Graham Barnard. However, various other people have also checked them for me from time-to-time – our usual *Treasure Quest* newsreader, Jim Cassidy, is very good for shooting down any nonsense!

As an example of how it all works, here's how the clue which led to Helhoughton in this particular week's programme all came together:

Bob's place is put alongside,
What doesn't compare to an angry woman.
Where there is a licence but no publican,
Go behind to find the clue.

- *Bob's place is put alongside = Bob as in Robert Walpole, his residence was Houghton Hall.*
- *What doesn't compare to an angry woman = as in "Hell hath no fury like a woman scorned," so Hell-Houghton, sounds like "Helhoughton".*
- *Where there is a licence but no publican = fully-licensed bar in the village hall.*
- *Go behind to find the clue = clue will be behind the bar.*

It's usually sometime on a Friday when I let Becky and Ian know where their starting point is going to be. On Sunday itself, I am at the studios bright and early to help produce the *Sunday Breakfast* programme before *Treasure Quest*, so I am able to hand Becky her copy of clue one, and to do a signal test with them once they have arrived at the starting point. This week I had chosen to start them in Great Palgrave, just north of Swaffham, as I knew we would get a good signal from that area. *Treasure Quest* takes advantage of the network of radio car receivers we have across the county (West Lynn, Great Massingham, West Runton, Norwich and Great Yarmouth), although we do sometimes stray into areas where unfortunately we don't get radio car reception!

Despite Becky's best efforts, this week's Quest ended in narrow failure!

We did have the radio car this particular week – a heavily-customised Peugeot 806 for those of you who are interested in such things – but as regular listeners will know, it's not always entirely reliable! So we have also used various other BBC vehicles from time-to-time down the years, into which we can sling assorted portable transmitters and various other bits of kit. Recently we have also been able to use a very clever system called 'LuciLive', which allows us to broadcast in high quality using the 3G mobile phone network. But as you may have noticed, usually when the worst comes to the worst and we cannot contact Becky in any other way, we have to fall back on good old-fashioned mobile phones. There are some parts of Norfolk where even these don't work, occasionally leaving us in something of a black hole!

Don't forget that if you have an idea for somewhere you would like to see used as a *Treasure Quest* location, you can always e-mail me at treasurequest@bbc.co.uk, or write to The Questmaster, BBC Radio Norfolk, The Forum, Millennium Plain, Norwich, NR2 1BH. Just make sure that you *never* send your suggestions to David, Becky or Ian – otherwise we won't be able to use them!

9

The Treasure Quest Treasury

Here is just a small selection, in A to Z form, of a few of the best and most interesting people, places, facts, stories and other miscellanea from across the nigh-on 200 episodes of *Treasure Quest* that have so far been transmitted on BBC Radio Norfolk.

A – Anneka Rice

During the 1980s and early 1990s, Anneka Rice was one of the biggest stars on British television. She became one of the country's best-known presenters through her work on *Challenge Anneka* for the BBC and, before that, *Treasure Hunt* for Channel 4. *Treasure Hunt*, which she fronted from 1982 until 1988, saw her searching for clues around a certain area of the country each episode, on behalf of two members of the public who had to solve these clues back in the studio. The programme was a massive success, drawing incredible audiences of up to seven million for Channel 4, and such was its status that Anneka remains a household name over two decades after the end of the show's run.

Given the similarities between *Treasure Hunt* and our own *Treasure*

Anneka Rice joins the team, on Valentine's Day 2010.

Quest, it wasn't very long before Becky Betts was being referred to in some quarters as Norfolk's answer to Anneka Rice, and it was often jokingly suggested on the show that perhaps she and Anneka ought to join forces. Listeners would frequently suggest the same thing, wanting Anneka and Becky to get together – presumably in a similar manner to one of those old episodes

Anneka takes a ride in the BBC Radio Norfolk radio car!

of *Doctor Who* where they all used to meet up!

After hearing that Anneka might perhaps sometimes be found staying on the North Norfolk coast, in the summer of 2009 the Questmaster decided to see whether it might be at all possible to involve her in the programme. He managed to track down the details of her personal assistant, who replied that she thought it was possible Anneka would want to be involved, but it was just a question of finding an opportunity in her schedule. The Questmaster's boss, Martyn Weston, eventually took over the negotiations and suddenly, in early February 2010, came a bolt from the blue. Anneka *would* be happy to take part in an edition of *Treasure Quest*... that coming Valentine's Day!

With only just over a week to put the show together, and only knowing a few days before transmission at what point in the show Anneka would actually be available, the Questmaster managed to put together a route that covered all eventualities and enabled Anneka to join in the fun for the longest possible time during the programme. All of this went on with David and Becky knowing absolutely nothing.

The great morning came and they eventually found a clue which seemed to be leading to someone who had been treasure hunting before. David wondered whether it might be Anneka who was waiting for Becky at Norwich Castle, where the clue was taking them, but Becky dismissed the idea – even commenting that she didn't want Anneka to turn up, as she'd put her to shame by looking "all skinny and blonde!" When Becky did eventually reach the castle and found Anneka waiting for her, her reaction was one of the most extraordinary displays of emotion ever heard during *Treasure Quest*. Screaming and even crying with excitement, Becky could hardly believe her eyes, shrieking at innocent members of the public from the top of the Castle Mound that she was in the presence of "Anneka *flipping* Rice!"

Although Anneka described the whole *Treasure Quest* team as being "completely mad," she was happy enough to roll back the years and join in the fun, teaming up with Becky to find clue five in the castle and then heading back to the BBC Radio Norfolk studios to get the treasure. This was particularly exciting for David Clayton as it meant he got the chance to meet her as well, with Anneka and Becky breathlessly racing into the studio against the clock in one of the most exciting and dramatic finishes ever to a *Treasure Quest* programme.

"What a present for Norfolk!" David declared of the show's Valentine's Day surprise, and the event was even reported by *The Guardian* newspaper on their website! Anneka wasn't put off by Becky's unique brand of enthusiasm, and later recorded a special video message to the team for that year's *Treasure Quest Live!* event in November.

In a programme with a long history of surprising twists and turns, the moment when Anneka joined in has become one of the best-remembered. The clip of Becky meeting "Anneka *flipping* Rice!" has certainly been given a fair few airings on BBC Radio Norfolk since February 2010!

B – Bawsey church ruins

Treasure Quest does not always find itself in locations which are still in one piece. Just as interesting to visit can be places long since abandoned, where the march of history has seen the people that once lived, worked or worshipped there move on, leaving to the elements the buildings they once occupied. Such is the case with the church at Bawsey, near King's Lynn, a rather picturesque ruin which stands atop a hill like a ghost, silently and solemnly observing the passage of the years.

Originally the church was dedicated to St James, and was part of a thriving village community at Bawsey. However, sometime during the 16th century the owner of the land decided that it would be far more profitable if the village were destroyed and the site left open for keeping livestock. With the type of decision that would later become infamous during the Highland Clearances of 19th century Scotland, the village was removed and the area turned into farmland.

Whether for religious reasons or otherwise, though, the church itself was not pulled down, but left alone at the top of the hill, where over the following centuries it gradually crumbled into the beautiful ruin which stands there now. These days the site is located in the middle of the aptly-named Church Farm, although it is accessible via a dirt trackway which runs up the side of the hill.

It was this trackway which almost brought *Treasure Quest* grinding to a halt during the programme's visit in March 2010. Stand-in 'runner' Kirsteen Thorne had managed to find the clue in among the ruins, although she and Navigator Ian had a slightly nervy time on their way up there as the radio car bumped its way along the track and through a couple of very deep puddles. Having made it up safely, once the clue had been found and Ian and Kirsteen were ready to come down they were committed to going back through the puddles... and this time the radio car decided enough was enough, choking to a halt!

Kirsteen Thorne interviews the clue holder at Bawsey, against the backdrop of the church ruins.

It seemed as if all was lost, but eventually – after some gentle persuasion! – the car managed to get the water out of its system and gurgled its way back into life. Navigator Ian, though, was probably somewhat more cautious about taking it through any puddles for the next few weeks!

There have been two occasions when the programme hasn't been quite so fortunate, with the radio car breaking down mid-show and stopping the Quest at Acle in June 2008 and at Wroxham in September 2009. There have also been programmes where the radio car has broken down earlier in the week and gone in for repair, so a variety of other BBC Radio Norfolk vehicles have been pressed into service down the years and jury-rigged with various lash-ups of different bits of broadcasting equipment – including Navigator Ian's personal favourite, the radio Land Rover!

Such is the BBC Radio Norfolk radio car's fame that it even represented radio cars as a whole in the 2011 edition of Michelin's *i-Spy* series book *Every Vehicle on the Road* – surely, no less than it deserves!

C – Castles

Being an historic county, Norfolk is fairly littered with castles of various different styles and periods, and in varying states of repair. Some, such as Norwich's, still stand imposingly on the landscape, while others *Treasure Quest* has visited, such as those at New Buckenham or Mileham, are now ruins, but no less fascinating for it.

The famous Norman castle that dominates the centre of Norwich, easily visible from the BBC Radio Norfolk offices, has been the site of several *Treasure Quest* clues. Probably its highest-profile role in the programme came on Valentine's Day 2010, when clue five was hidden there with a replica of the famous prehistoric artefact the Happisburgh Handaxe, although all that was rather forgotten given that also waiting there for Becky was a certain Anneka Rice!

Castle Rising in West Norfolk, near to King's Lynn, has also been a *Treasure Quest* location on more than one occasion. On October 31st 2010 it held one of the clues for a Halloween Special, when all of the locations that day were associated with particular ghostly legends or Halloween-related objects. The story goes that Queen Isabella, the wife of King Edward II in the 14th century, was imprisoned in the castle after she had murdered the King, taken another man as her lover and briefly seized control of the country.

Her son, King Edward III, deposed her but could not bring himself to have her executed, hence the exile to Castle Rising, where she spent the rest of her days. The tale has it that she eventually went mad there, roaming the upper storeys, and that her ghostly screams can still be heard to this day. Becky Betts, however, was not particularly impressed when the Questmaster went to great lengths to broadcast a scream sound effect over the airwaves during her visit. Becky was not upset by it at all! On this occasion, the scream came not from a ghost, but was recorded from the more earthly vocal chords of BBC East journalist Harriet Morter!

Becky has also visited one castle belonging to another county, when she found one of her clues at Bungay Castle in Suffolk in December 2008. Once she was there she wasn't entirely sure where she had to head next, so ended up leading a parade of local listeners around the streets of the town like some East Anglian equivalent of the Pied Piper!

Other castles to have been visited by *Treasure Quest* down the years include the aforementioned New Buckenham and Mileham ruins; Burgh Castle, near Great Yarmouth, which featured in the second pilot programme on the May Bank Holiday of 2008; the Castle Acre ruins north of Swaffham – location of *Treasure Quest*'s first ever treasure! – and, while not quite a castle, the site of the iron age fort at Tasburgh in South Norfolk is also of historical importance, and was a treasure location in March 2009.

So *Treasure Quest* has certainly made its way around Norfolk's historic castles and forts. And although it's rarely safe to predict anything with this particular programme, it seems unlikely the show has visited its last such location just yet!

D – HMS *Dauntless*

Norfolk hasn't had a Royal Navy vessel named for the county since the most recent HMS *Norfolk* – the fifth so far to have borne the name since 1693 – was sold to the Chilean navy in 2006, where she now sails under the name of *Almirante Cochrane*. This isn't to say the county doesn't maintain its traditional strong links with the 'senior service' though, and in October 2010 the type 45 destroyer HMS *Dauntless* was officially 'affiliated' with the town of Great Yarmouth. At the time, *Dauntless* was the Royal Navy's newest vessel, having only been commissioned in June 2010, and as part of the affiliation ceremonies the ship travelled down from Crombie in Scotland to the also-new outer harbour at Yarmouth, where it spent several days docked, allowing local people to come on board and tour the ship.

The week before the *Dauntless*'s arrival in Yarmouth, the Questmaster took a call during *Treasure Quest* from a listener called Jean, from Gorleston, who suggested to him that it would be a perfect clue or treasure location for the programme. The Questmaster was particularly taken with the idea as he knows there's little that excites Becky Betts more than a man in uniform, so the notion of her encountering a shipload of Royal Navy sailors was too good to resist! A few phone calls during the week saw its use on *Treasure Quest* quickly arranged, and Becky was indeed particularly excited when the day came and she realised where it was she had to go for her final location.

Although Becky was able to find the treasure envelope in good time, located with a fire-fighting suit in the ship's helicopter hangar, there was a disappointment for her at the end of this Quest. Most of the crew were away parading through Yarmouth to celebrate the ship's affiliation with the town, leaving only a skeleton crew back on board. And nice and charming though she was, Lieutenant Ellie Berry – who had the task of looking after Becky – wasn't *quite* what our intrepid

Becky finds herself all at sea aboard HMS Dauntless at Great Yarmouth's outer harbour in October 2010. But at least she got the treasure in time!

Quester had been hoping for!

It does have to be said, though, that Becky has had plenty of men in uniform to keep her happy during the course of *Treasure Quest*. In March 2009 she found one of her clues at RAF Marham, the airbase in West Norfolk, where she met Wing Commander Simon Ellard, who told her they would let her into the base because she had announced she'd put extra lip gloss on!

Becky meets a man in uniform! Wing Commander Simon Ellard at RAF Marham, March 2009.

The following year, as part of the Easter 2010 two-parter, Becky was led to the guardroom of Robertson Barracks at Swanton Morley, the home of the army's Light Dragoons, the modern-day successors of one of the regiments that took part in the Charge of the Light Brigade. There she found her clue with Captain Lenny Newcombe and some of his soldiers on guard duty – although when she had the clue, they ended up locking her inside one of the guardroom cells until she had solved it! Surrounded by the uniformed men, though, Becky wasn't entirely unhappy – and she was even more pleased when, later in the year, she got her hands on two Dragoons when they were mystery 'Guess the Guests' at *Treasure Quest Live!*

It's not just the armed forces that Becky enjoys mixing with – the uniformed emergency services will do just as nicely. Hence she was equally pleased to be sent to retrieve a clue from the training building at North Earlham Fire Station at Easter 2009, and also to encounter many policemen during the *Treasure Quest* which took place entirely around the Royal Norfolk Showground on Police Gala Day in August 2008.

E – Emneth

Far out on the distant western edge of Norfolk, almost as far as you can go in the county without falling off into Cambridgeshire, sits the village of Emneth. Just on the right side of Wisbech, Emneth perches rather unobtrusively on its ledge of Norfolk, perhaps just a little cut off from the world, having lost its connection to the railway in 1968 as part of the Beeching Axe.

This latter fact could be considered particularly unfortunate given the reason that a *Treasure Quest* clue was located in the village in May 2010. The Questmaster had written a riddle which led Becky to St Edmund's, the parish church. Nothing too unusual in that; *Treasure Quest* has featured churches all across Norfolk during its run, with clues located in fonts, with particular pieces of stonework or statues, and even – much to Becky's chagrin! – up the occasional tower.

In this case, the clue was located with one of the stained glass windows in the church. This window is unusual in that it doesn't commemorate a saint or an angel or indeed any kind of religious figure. Instead, it depicts the legendary children's story character of Thomas the Tank Engine, for the very good reason that many of the books featuring Thomas were written in Emneth, when their author, the Reverend W. Awdry, was vicar of the parish between 1953 and 1965.

As is all too often the case with *Treasure Quest*, there wasn't time to go into this fascinating little bit of local history in any detail during the programme itself. However, a few weeks later the Reverend Awdry's former church warden, 'Dobbie' Carr, visited the studio in the 'Quest Guest' slot on David and Becky's Friday show. She spent an involving twenty minutes or so relating her memories of the man and his work, the great honour it was to be allowed to change the points on his grand train set in the vicarage attic, and how the Reverend was inspired by local features such as the old steam tram running down the main road, which became 'Toby the Tram Engine'. David Clayton, though, was most interested by Dobbie's nickname, and wondered what her real name might be – "I've got a real name which nobody knows and I don't repeat!" came the reply!

The Emneth episode just goes to show one of the things *Treasure Quest* is best at – finding fascinating stories tucked away in the county where we live. Who would have thought that a character loved by millions of children the world over had his adventures penned in a small Norfolk vicarage?

Becky on the beach at Sea Palling in February 2011, having been led there by a famous story about oranges!

F – Fruit

Or, more specifically in this case, oranges. One show in February 2011 saw Becky having to find a clue in the medical kit of the Sea Palling lifeboat, on the east coast of the county. This turned out to be an adventure in and of itself, as Becky had to get her feet wet retrieving the clue from the lifeboat as it returned to the beach after exercising off shore. She ended up uttering an expletive on-air after she twice managed to drop the clue in the sea!

But it was the clue that led to Sea Palling which perhaps had the more interesting story to tell. To get them to this particular village, the Questmaster decided to make reference to a famous event that occurred there in December 1948. A merchant ship called the *Bosphorous* ran into trouble just off the coast, on Haisborough Sands, and ended up jettisoning its cargo of oranges.

Hundreds of crates of oranges, as well as thousands of loose ones, ended up being beached all along the nearby coastline, with a particular concentration at Sea Palling, which became a centre for the unauthorised local "salvage" operation which followed! Having just gone through the Second World War, and with rationing still in place, many people in this part of Norfolk had never even seen an orange before. This unexpected arrival proved wildly popular and drew hundreds of people to the coast to collect their own share!

It was, in many ways, like a Norfolk-based version of the film *Whiskey Galore!*, only with less alcohol, and far too good a local yarn to be only touched on briefly during *Treasure Quest*. Graham Barnard therefore made the story the subject of his phone-in on the following edition of *Treasure Quest: Extra Time*. It turned out that a great many listeners not only knew the story but remembered it happening, and called in with their tales.

Ray in Smallburgh told how his father gathered enough of the oranges to box up and send to his fiancée in Leeds, clearly winning her heart and ensuring that Ray later came along! Barry from Norwich was a child at the time and was amazed when one of his friends came to school one day with bags of oranges, which none of he or his classmates had ever seen before – his friend's father had taken his own boat out and collected several boxes of them! Barry and his friends didn't even know at first that you had to take the skin off to eat them! Mary in Acle also phoned Graham to say how her mother ended up using the fruity gift from the sea to make "gallons and gallons" of orange wine, after her father had gone down to the beach and brought a load back in a pram! And Kathleen called to relate how some desiccated coconut was also washed ashore in the same shipwreck; "the first four or five inches were soaked in seawater, but the middle bit was all right!"

G – Great Hockham

The very name of Great Hockham is something of a misnomer, as it suggests that there is a Little Hockham to go with it. In fact, what was once Little Hockham is now virtually deserted, and the parish of Hockham is, to all intents and purposes, made up solely of the 'Great' part. The village sits on the edge of the Breckland, eight miles to the north of Thetford, and while at first glance you may think there is little to distinguish it from many other Norfolk villages, there is a good reason why it has its own entry here.

Great Hockham is noteworthy because it has a stone. And not just any old stone, either. Estimated to weigh somewhere in the region of three or four tonnes, this mighty lump of sandstone was discovered in the 19th century in a place called 'High Field', between the Shropham and Harling Roads in the village. The stone had been picked up from somewhere in Lincolnshire by a glacier many thousands of years beforehand, and when the glacier had had enough of it, it deposited it in this quiet little corner of Norfolk.

But that was not to be the end of the stone's journey. Nobody knows exactly when – nor, indeed, why – but sometime around about the year 1880, a villager by the name of John Pinner, a local farmer and proprietor of Pinners Bakers and Groceries on the Watton Road, decided that the stone should be in a more central location. He therefore had it dragged to the village green, where it has sat ever since and become the focus of a unique local ceremony.

Starting with Queen Victoria's golden jubilee in 1887, the villagers of Great Hockham decided that the perfect way to commemorate occasions of great national import would be to raise the stone... and then to put it back down again the other way up. According to the village website, this was first done using two horses harnessed to it with chains or ropes. More recently, it has been achieved by a team of villagers gradually shoring it up with wood until it reaches a crucial

Stand-in 'runner' Sophie Price meets some locals at Great Hockham's famous stone in September 2008.

balancing point and then goes over, coming thudding down the other way up and leaving a flattened patch of grass next to it.

The stone was next turned in 1897 for Victoria's diamond jubilee, then again in 1902 – either to mark the end of the Boer War or to celebrate the coronation of King Edward VII, it's not certain which – and again in 1911 (for the coronation of King George V), 1937 (the coronation of King George VI), 1977 (Queen Elizabeth II's silver jubilee), 1995 (the 50th anniversary of VE Day), 2000 (the millennium celebrations), 2002 (the Queen's golden jubilee) and most recently in 2008 (to mark the defeat of a planning application which would have seen the loss of local woodland). It is next due to be turned in 2012, as part of the celebrations of the Queen's diamond jubilee.

Treasure Quest visited the site in September 2008, when stand-in 'runner' Sophie Price found her second clue of the morning there and learned the stone's fascinating history from some of the villagers. An interesting story of a tradition peculiar to Norfolk, and another of the many intriguing tales from local history the programme has highlighted down the years.

H – Helicopters

That programme with which *Treasure Quest* is so often compared, Channel 4's *Treasure Hunt*, was all about criss-crossing the country by helicopter. So it's hardly surprising that, almost ever since the start of the show's run, it had been suggested both by listeners and members of staff at BBC Radio Norfolk that Becky should be sent up in a helicopter one week. There was only one slight problem with this: Becky's oft-expressed fear of flying!

Nevertheless, when the Questmaster was contacted by Joanne Brown from a local company called Sterling Helicopters in the summer of 2009, the opportunity was too much for him to resist. Joanne was a fan of *Treasure Quest* and had heard Becky mention her dread of being sent up in a helicopter – so was offering the Questmaster the chance to make her do just that!

The flight was originally planned for June 2009 at the Muckleburgh Collection military vehicle museum in North Norfolk, but the clues were not solved quickly that day. As the radio car was needed for another programme later in the afternoon, *Treasure Quest*

A pensive-looking Becky Betts prepares to go flying, October 2009.

couldn't spill over into the next show. So instead the Questmaster kept what would have been the finale that week a secret, until eventually another opportunity came up later in the year. So it came to pass that on October 11th 2009, the listeners unravelled a clue that Becky realised was sending her to Norwich Airport, and her date with destiny.

It was always made very clear to Becky that if she genuinely did not want to go up she didn't have to, and Ian could do it for her. However, in spite of her very-real tears and trauma as she got to the airport, a phone call from her mother during a record persuaded her that she

Becky and pilot Stewart Milner enjoy some celebratory cake at Dunston Hall after her second – rather more traumatic! – Treasure Quest helicopter adventure, on Easter Monday 2010.

needed to pull herself together and face her fear. With *Treasure Quest* listeners gathering outside the airport to wave and show their support, Becky went up and down for a short flight, and to her immense surprise even ended up enjoying it! So much so that when she got back to the BBC Radio Norfolk studios afterwards, she *almost* hugged the Questmaster – he only just managed to duck out of the way in time!

The fact that the flight had gone so well led the Questmaster and his boss Martyn Weston to hatch a devious plan when they were looking for a big finish to the *Treasure Quest* Easter 2010 two-part special. Becky had only gone up and down for a short 'hop' on her first helicopter flight – what if, to find the treasure on Easter Monday, she actually had to go on a little journey from one location to another...?

Everything was arranged with Sterling Helicopters and Dunston Hall, which was to be the location of the treasure, but the big question was whether it was actually technically possible to broadcast live from a helicopter. It was decided that it was worth a go, and the BBC's Steve Parks – or 'Engineer Steve' as he's been known to the listenership when he's helped *Treasure Quest* out on various occasions – was able to fit a small portable transmitter to the helicopter, so that once Becky was up and airborne, the listeners could hear every moment of her journey.

And what a journey it was – Becky's tears, rants at David, worries over turbulence and requests for tissues during her brief flight certainly left a remarkable impression on the BBC Radio Norfolk audience. Some felt it was awful to have sent her up again, while others thought it was the funniest or most dramatic piece of radio they had heard for years. It certainly got the biggest reaction of anything *Treasure Quest* has ever done – from Becky and from the listeners!

One thing is for certain, though – after the helicopter had landed, the tears had dried and the special 100th Quest celebratory cake had been eaten, Becky made the Questmaster promise he would never send her flying ever again. He's kept his word – so far!

Becky prepares to go into bat at Horsford, June 2010.

I – Innings

As she herself would be the first to admit, Becky Betts isn't the sportiest of characters. Usually, having to run to fetch a clue or the treasure solicits all manner of complaints from her, so it's perhaps none too surprising that she wasn't massively keen when, in June 2010, she was sent after runs of a different kind. The listeners had unravelled one of Questmaster's clues and revealed that it was leading her to Manor Park, the cricket ground at Horsford, just to the north of Norwich.

Manor Park is the home not just of Horsford Cricket Club, but also of the Norfolk county team. On the day she was there Becky "only" had to face a bowler from the Horsford under-9s, but she still had to get fully kitted-up in protective helmet and pads, not the most flattering of looks she has ever donned!

Nonetheless, despite barely being able to see through the helmet and with all the protection somewhat inhibiting any chance to display an athletic grace, Becky was able to actually hit the ball which was launched in her direction by one of the young players. She surprised David, the Questmaster and all of the listeners with a very satisfying "thwack" of leather on willow, before running – or perhaps more accurately, waddling! – down the wicket to retrieve her clue.

Cricket is by no means the only sport Becky has had to try before she's been allowed a clue or a treasure. Among others, she's also had to attempt – and failed badly at – potting a ball during a 24-hour snooker marathon in Lessingham; gone ten-pin bowling at Great Yarmouth's Wellington Pier; thrown a foam javelin at the Rudham Festival mini-Olympics event; been putting at Gorleston Golf Club; played softball in Hoveton; had to join in with training exercises at North Walsham Rugby Club in Scottow and the Fakenham Foxes ladies' team; and she's had to have a go at taking a penalty at West Lynn Ladies FC.

On the subject of football, probably her least enjoyable sport-related task came in November 2010, when she had to try and find her treasure in a pub full of over-excited Norwich City fans an hour before kick-off in the big East Anglian Derby game against Ipswich Town. An uncomfortable experience for Becky because, being a Suffolk girl, she's an Ipswich fan, and all the Norwich fans seemed to know it! She was even less impressed when she eventually got hold of the treasure – a Norwich City scarf – and had stern words with the Questmaster following that particular episode!

J – Job swap

A question often posed to the programme by the listeners, from quite soon into the life of *Treasure Quest*, was "why don't you make David and Becky swap places one week?" This idea was particularly keenly taken up by Nick Conrad, who incited the audience to get behind his "campaign" to make the swap happen when he compèred *Treasure Quest Live!* in November 2009, and then made his desire to see the switch occur a feature of his 'Treasure Quest: Extra Time' hour in the

David finally goes Treasure Questing, in February 2010.

show following *Treasure Quest*. He managed to get many of the listeners to text and call in with their support for the notion, and it quickly became a matter of only 'when' rather than 'if' it would occur.

When it finally did, in February 2010, the most important thing was that David Clayton was to know absolutely nothing about it. Becky Betts was kept hidden out of his way as the programme started, and David assumed she was off and about in parts unknown with Ian and the radio car. In fact, they were parked just outside the BBC Radio Norfolk studios, and as David went to the first record, she and Ian made their way indoors. As soon as the song came to an end, David crossed back to her to find out where she was, and into the studio they came – much to David's shock and amazement!

David has been working in radio for so long and faced so many different situations during his broadcasting career that he is very rarely lost for words. But when the Questmaster informed him that Becky was in the studio because she would be handling the maps that morning, while he was to go out with Ian in the radio car to find the clues, he was well and truly flabbergasted!

Nonetheless, out he went, and he even managed to find the treasure. He did have one or two uncomfortable moments along the way, such as having to pick one clue from a tray of maggots in a bait shop at Barford Lakes. But some listeners felt that he had been given rather too easy a time of it on the whole, compared to what Becky usually has to put up with. So perhaps one day the Questmaster will swap them over again, and try and give David some more difficult tasks to undertake!

David and Becky aren't the only members of the regular team to have done someone else's job on the show. As well as Alexajain Wills-

72

Bradfield having stood-in as the Questmistress on Boxing Day 2010, David took a Sunday off in April that year and the Questmaster took his place as the studio presenter – a rare instance of he and Becky actually being on the same side for a change!

Out and about: in July 2011 the Questmaster swapped roles with Becky to have a go at finding the clues.

Becky and the Questmaster were on opposing sides but in a different way to usual for one programme in July 2011, when he went out and about finding the clues in the radio car, while Becky produced the show in the studio – and both found a new appreciation for how difficult the other one's job can be at times! The Questmaster narrowly failed to find the treasure that day, much to Becky's delight as she provided a gloating countdown with the final location almost in sight!

K – King's Lynn

As you'd expect given its position as one of Norfolk's largest and most important towns, King's Lynn has seen its fair share of *Treasure Quest*. There have been clues located at the historic Custom House; at the Corn Exchange, where Becky had to get to grips with Norfolk wrestling star and TV Gladiator Nick Aldis; with some Civil War re-enactors on Purfleet Quay; and she also had to find a clue with a picture of herself on a board displaying local celebrities at the Green Quay environment centre. Probably her most memorable visit to the town, though, was when she had to go there to do a spot of ghost hunting!

The Tudor Rose Hotel, just off the town's historic Tuesday Market Place, was the location for the dramatic finale of *Treasure Quest*'s special Halloween episode in October 2010. As the show fell on the 31st, the Questmaster had associated most of the locations with local ghost stories. The Tudor Rose, built around the year 1500, is the home of a particularly well-known Norfolk ghost story, about a phantom bride known only as 'The Grey Lady'.

Nobody knows who this lady was or when exactly she died, only that she apparently appears to certain guests in the form of a woman in a wedding dress. The story is told that she is the restless spirit of a newly-wed bride, who was murdered in the hotel by her husband on the very night of their nuptials. The Grey Lady is most often reputed to haunt room seven at the Tudor Rose, the room where she supposedly met her grisly fate. It must be said, though, that when BBC Radio Norfolk's Stephen Bumfrey stayed in the room for a Halloween special of his programme in 2007, he claimed to have enjoyed the best night's sleep he's ever had!

When the Questmaster arranged with the Tudor Rose to have the treasure envelope located in room seven, he was delighted to discover that a group offering ghost walks around King's Lynn had their very own 'Grey Lady' who would be prepared to play the part especially for Becky's visit. When Becky arrived with only a few minutes to spare at the end of the episode, she was already unsettled by the unusual cold around the room. When she then ventured inside to find the treasure, she was somewhat more than unsettled when confronted with the 'Grey Lady' – in full blood-stained wedding dress and deathly pale make-up – looming out at her through the door of the en-suite bathroom!

Becky let out a terrified shriek and refused to go back into the room, even after she had been reassured that the apparition was actually a friendly lady called Natalie. She sent Navigator Ian back in for the treasure, and could barely bring herself to even look at Natalie in her make-up and costume!

L – Lincolnshire

BBC Radio Norfolk is, by its very nature, a local radio station. Although we always like to make sure our listeners aren't cut off from the rest of the world and we do our best to keep them up to date with the latest national and international news and events, we are primarily concerned with radio made by, for and about the people of Norfolk. And that almost always means, as you might expect, broadcasting from within the borders of the county.

But every now and again, only very occasionally when we think that nobody's looking and we can probably just about get away with it,

Treasure Quest likes to briefly run across the border and then come back again. Almost like a young child doing a dare, and then maintaining an expression of perfect innocence afterwards. "What? Leave Norfolk? Us? No, never! Must have been another radio programme..."

L is for Lincolnshire because that was

On the edge: the radio car at Ness Point, in Lowestoft, Suffolk, in September 2009.

the first place we visited on an extra-Norfolk excursion, when Becky found a clue at the church in Long Sutton in October 2008. In fairness that is only *just* over the border, so close that we even found we have listeners there, but it still came as a surprise and Becky was rather nervous about the idea of crossing over into "foreign" territory – even asking whether she ought to have packed her passport!

Since then the Questmaster has become a little more daring, and allowed clues or even treasure to be placed in other counties on a few further occasions, so that the programme has now visited all of Norfolk's three neighbours. Suffolk has been visited on a handful of occasions – such as having a clue located at Ness Point in Lowestoft, the most easterly tip of the British mainland, in September 2009; a treasure at the Norfolk & Suffolk Aviation Museum in Flixton, near Bungay, in January 2011; and a clue at the top of Beccles Bell Tower in June 2011.

Cambridgeshire has only properly been visited once, in December 2009, when Becky had to find a clue at the Octavia Hill Birthplace Museum in Wisbech. This was a memorable clue location as, to claim the clue from the Mayor of Wisbech, Becky had to interrupt (by special arrangement of the Questmaster!) a full-scale lecture on Octavia Hill's life which was taking place in the museum at the time!

Something of an argument broke out among the listenership in March 2011, when Becky had a clue leading her to Outwell, on the very western edge of Norfolk. It was clear she had to find the shop belonging to Peter Carter, the last of the traditional Fenland eel-catchers, but nobody could seem to agree on whether or not Outwell was in Norfolk or Cambridgeshire. Consultation with the villagers after Becky had found the clue eventually led to the conclusion that while part of Outwell had indeed once been in Cambridgeshire, these days the entirety of the village was officially in Norfolk... just!

M – Maps

The Questmaster models one of the maps David is allowed to use!

In the early days, Becky and Ian were rather spoiled with the use of "navigational aids" in their pursuit of the treasure. As well as being allowed to use the map kept in the radio car for the use of other shows, on the original *Treasure Quest* pilot they also had the benefit of Navigator Ian's own satellite navigation device. It was quickly decided that GPS made things far too easy for them, and a short way into the regular run of the programme in the summer of 2008, they were also banned from looking at their own map – much to Becky's irritation!

It had been decided that it was far more fun to let David Clayton and the listeners of Norfolk guide Becky around the county, using the airwaves as a kind of personalised, broadcast GPS system purely for the benefit of the radio car team! This usually works very well, although it has been found down the years that as soon as one listener phones in and gives the team some very confident and clear directions to a location, the switchboard will immediately light up with people claiming "No no no, you don't want to go *that* way, *this* way's much quicker..."

For those of you who take an interest in such things, the two maps the Questmaster usually issues to David at the start of each programme are a large-scale, fold-out 'Norfolk Navigator' to give a view of the whole county, and a more detailed, spiral-bound 'Street Atlas' of Norfolk, for a closer-in view of any given town or village. The street atlas has lasted since the start of the show's run, although David has often been heard to complain that a location is in the gap between two of its pages!

The larger maps have proven somewhat more fragile, with David gradually tearing apart three Norfolk Navigators before he was given his beloved laminated copy in October 2010. This was a present from a *Treasure Quest* fan, who happened to stumble across the National Map Centre in London one day, and commissioned them to make the laminated, and thus now indestructible, Norfolk Navigator, just for David. David also has some sticky coloured arrows he likes to place onto the map to chart Becky and Ian's progress during the show as if he were plotting the Battle of Britain, which were also a gift from a listener.

As any regular follower of the show will know, however, Becky doesn't have enormous faith in David's abilities as a map reader, and has often blamed him for failing to get the treasure in time. She also frequently lambasts his ability to actually fold his Norfolk Navigator map properly, something which has become such a sore point between the two of them that at the *Treasure Quest Live!* stage shows in 2009 and 2010, several

David's special map-reading certificate and badge from the Norwich Sea Scouts. He's very proud of these!

audience members were cajoled into taking part in men's and women's map-folding competitions to see who was the best at it!

David doesn't *always* have the same maps, however. Very occasionally the Questmaster likes to pull a bit of a switch, such as the week when David was only allowed some replica 19th century maps of Norfolk, donated by BBC Radio Norfolk's news editor, Nicky Barnes. And it's not just printed maps which help David. He, and all of our listeners with an internet connection, have access to a very clever satellite tracker located on the BBC Norfolk website. This handy little device, the brainchild of the BBC Norfolk website team's Martin Barber in early 2009, allows listeners at home to see exactly where the radio car is, and where it's heading, at any given time during the show. The tracker unit is also occasionally loaned out for other uses at the station – most notably when it was on the boat following BBC Radio Norfolk producer David Webster during his cross-channel swim in September 2010!

For a time there was also a live webcam fixed to the top of the radio car so listeners could follow its progress on the website. However, it often ended up showing an image of a squashed insect that had been unfortunate enough to collide with the camera while the car was moving!

N – Nelson

The Questmaster was once heard to quip during the programme that his time researching clue locations for *Treasure Quest* down the years had taught him two certain facts about Norfolk. The first was that every town in the county has seemingly had a great fire which burned the place to the ground at some point in its history. The second was that every town in Norfolk claims that Nelson went to school there.

A slight exaggeration, perhaps, but there is no doubting that Norfolk is proud of being the birthplace of Britain's most celebrated naval hero. Of course, this means that Lord Horatio has cropped up during *Treasure Quest* on more than one occasion.

In October 2010, Becky found one of her clues with a mannequin of the man himself at the Norfolk Nelson Museum, located on the South Quay in Great Yarmouth. The coastal town is particularly proud of its association with Nelson, as it was to Yarmouth that Nelson first returned to England after his victory over the French at the Battle of the Nile. He was given the freedom of the borough, an honour even Becky Betts has not yet been accorded.

The Museum also looks after the 19th century monument to Nelson which is located on the Denes in Yarmouth. Norfolk's very own version of Nelson's Column, it pre-dates its more famous cousin in Trafalgar Square by over twenty years, having been completed in 1819. Known variously as the Nelson Monument, the Britannia Monument and the Norfolk Pillar, the 144-foot high column is topped with a statue of Britannia, with the regal ruler of the waves allegedly positioned so that she points towards Nelson's birthplace, Burnham Thorpe.

Becky looking triumphant after conquering the Britannia Monument in Great Yarmouth, in September 2008.

Knowing Becky's reluctance to ever go up high or climb a lot of stairs, the Questmaster took great delight in having the treasure for one Sunday's Quest in September 2008 positioned right at the top of the Monument. This gave rise to one of the most memorable sequences in *Treasure Quest*'s history, as Becky entered the doorway at the bottom of the column and exclaimed, in surprise and dismay, "It's a *spiral* staircase!" What other type of staircase she might have been expecting to find inside a column is unclear.

She eventually made it to the top, after much protest, groaning and gasping for breath. Although she could barely walk for some days afterwards, she did at least manage to bring herself to look out at the spectacular view, even if the height made her feel rather unwell! Probably the less said about the clue that actually led her to this

You'd have to be a real dummy not to get this one! The man himself guards the clue for us at the Norfolk Nelson Museum in Great Yarmouth, October 2010.

treasure the better – it referenced Nelson's wife, Fanny, and gave rise to one of David Clayton's favourite *Treasure Quest* bloopers as Becky frantically implored some innocent bystanders in Hopton to "name some famous Fannys!"

O – Ocean Room

Before David Clayton was a radio presenter he was a disc jockey, spinning the wheels of steel in various locations across Norfolk during the 1970s and early 1980s. Of all the venues where he stood behind the decks, the one with which he is most associated – and for which he probably retains the most affection – is the Ocean Room, a function suite located in his old home town of Gorleston. Opened in the 1930s as a dance venue called the Floral Hall, it was taken over by local businessman Gordon Edwards in the 1970s. He turned it into the Ocean Room, which it remains to this day.

David was master of the decks at the Ocean Room from the mid-1970s up until 1983, very much the Disco King of Norfolk. His stint at the venue lingered long in many memories – not least his! – and over the years listeners to his programmes on BBC Radio Norfolk have regularly been treated to anecdotes of his time there, which invariably begin with the well-worn phrase "When I was a DJ at the Ocean Room..."

Having noticed David's penchant for an Ocean Room story or two, the Questmaster decided it would be a nice idea to hide a clue there, and this was duly arranged for the end of one Quest in July 2008. However, it wasn't *quite* as simple as that. Having already solved five clues, Becky raced into the Ocean Room with the clock ticking down to the end of the programme, finding her usual brown envelope up on stage with the DJ decks where David once worked... Only to discover that it wasn't the treasure at all, but a sneaky sixth clue.

With no time to reach any other location all seemed lost, but the secret was in one of the Questmaster's favourite ever *Treasure Quest* anagrams, contained in this new clue. The phrase "Vinyl Data Doc", seemingly complete nonsense that may or may not have something to do with records, was eventually realised by a listener to be an anagram of none other than "David Clayton". David realised that the clue led to him having to reach under his chair back in the BBC Radio Norfolk studio and, after frantically throwing the chair over to grab the envelope, he found the treasure. The Questmaster had sellotaped it there earlier that morning, before David's arrival.

So it was David himself who found the treasure that particular week – and with just five seconds left on the clock, in one of *Treasure Quest*'s closest-ever finishes.

P – Pedlar of Swaffham

As well as anagrams, another element the Questmaster likes to include in his clues is local history – or, even better, local legends and folklore. There are many tall tales told of fantastic figures from the depths of history who have allegedly lived in or visited towns and villages across Norfolk, and one of the best known of these yarns is the story of the Pedlar of Swaffham. One of the best known, that is, unless you're occasional Becky Betts stand-in Sophie Price!

Sophie was having her first go at substituting for Becky in August 2008, when she found the final clue which led her in the direction of Swaffham. Quick-witted listeners had rapidly worked out that she needed to look for someone dressed up as the Pedlar of Swaffham, as part of a living history event that was taking place in the town that day. With time running out as the radio car headed towards the location, Sophie innocently asked David: "So this pedaller, he'll be in costume

Becky points out the pedlar on the Swaffham sign during a subsequent Treasure Quest visit to the town, in April 2009.

will he, on a bike?" This was much to David's amusement, and Sophie has never been allowed to forget it.

But perhaps she's not the only person who would have experienced this confusion – a pedlar being, rather than a cyclist, an old term for a travelling salesman, someone who went from town to town, village to village, hawking various goods. So, for those of you who are not familiar with it, here is the legend told locally of the famous Pedlar of Swaffham.

The story goes that, way back in the distant past, a pedlar who lived at Swaffham dreamed that if he were to visit London Bridge, he would learn some news there that would bring him great joy and good fortune. Initially the pedlar dismissed the dream as a mere fancy, but the dream came back again and again, night after night. Deciding that there was nothing else for it, he resolved to undertake the long journey to London, to go to the bridge and find out whether there was any truth in his premonition.

For two or three days the pedlar stayed on the bridge, keeping a close eye on all of the people and the shops and inns that clustered on the busy crossing. He looked hopefully at many of the passers-by, wondering whether this or that person might be the bringer of the unknown news, but none of the people there seemed to pay him any heed.

Just as the pedlar had decided that he had been a prize fool to come such a long way for nothing more than a dream, he was approached by one of the shopkeepers who worked on the bridge. This man had seen the pedlar standing about, and had noticed how he didn't appear to be there to buy or sell anything. The shopkeeper was curious as to what the pedlar was doing, and had now decided to ask.

When the pedlar explained about his dream, the shopkeeper laughed, clearly thinking him a country simpleton. "Why, last night I dreamed that I was in Swaffham, in the county of Norfolk, a place I never knew of in all my days!" the shopkeeper said – to which the pedlar kept quiet. "I dreamed that in that place I saw the house of a pedlar, and behind that house a mighty oak tree, under which a great treasure was buried. But you do not see me heading all the way to Norfolk simply because of a dream!"

The pedlar thanked the man and, without explaining, headed home to Swaffham as quickly as he could. There he dug beneath the oak tree that stood behind his house, and sure enough found a great treasure, buried there long ago by ancient persons unknown, which kept the pedlar and his family rich for the rest of their days. In thanks for his dream, the pedlar paid for Swaffham church, which had at this point in history fallen into disrepair, to be fully restored to its former glory.

So goes the story, at any rate. If nothing else, Swaffham has certainly provided the locations for at least half-a-dozen clues down the years, and it also holds one unique and very special place in the history of *Treasure Quest* on BBC Radio Norfolk. For it was in Swaffham that Becky and Ian started off the very first episode of the show, on Good Friday in 2008. So an historic town in more ways than one!

Q – Questmistress

David Clayton, Becky Betts and Ian Forster have all been present right from the very start of *Treasure Quest*, taking part in the one-off pilot episode broadcast at Easter 2008. That's not the case for the Questmaster, though. His first encounter with the programme was coming in later that day, as the first *Treasure Quest* was ending, to work on the following

The Questmistress revealed! BBC Radio Norfolk's Amy Barratt, the original producer of Treasure Quest.

programme presented by Chris Bailey. As he surveyed the exhausted scene in the 'ops room', the production area where the producer and telephone-answerers sit, he thought to himself: "Thank goodness I didn't have to work on that programme!"

The woman who did have to put the very first *Treasure Quest* together was producer Amy Barratt, now retrospectively known as the Questmistress. The 'Questmaster' title hadn't been thought of at the time – this was something David came up with at the beginning of the show's regular run, inspired by 'the Banker' on the Channel 4 game show *Deal or No Deal*.

Whatever her title, it was Amy's job to decide how exactly this *Treasure Quest* idea was going to work in Norfolk, where the best route would be for the very first Quest – which she even drove herself to test the times and deliver the clues – and of course she also had to write the cryptic riddles that would keep the people of Norfolk guessing. She made a great success of it, which is the reason why *Treasure Quest* took off and why it's still going strong today.

These days Amy works mainly as a journalist on the news desk at BBC Radio Norfolk, helping to prepare and read the hourly bulletins and setting up items for the breakfast and drive time shows. She also sometimes stands-in as the station's news editor, and deputises for Graham Barnard as the weekend programmes editor.

Prior to this Amy was one of the producers working on the programmes team at BBC Radio Norfolk, and for several years worked alongside the late Roy Waller, producing his mid-morning and afternoon shows. She has also been the producer of BBC Radio Norfolk's breakfast show. In addition to her behind-the-scenes talents, Amy has from time-to-time stood-in as a presenter for the station. While she was Roy's producer she would regularly deputise for him whenever he had to take a show off, and she has also presented other shows such as the drive time slot and the old Sunday dedications programme.

Although Amy didn't go on to produce *Treasure Quest* once it became a regular weekly show, she has made a couple of returns to her Questmistress role. In April 2010 David Clayton had taken a week off and it had been decided that the Questmaster should have a go at presenting in his place. There was, therefore, only one possible candidate to step into the Questmaster's shoes and put the programme together that week – the woman who had done the job before he did!

Additionally, in July 2011 Amy planned the route and wrote all the clues for the week when Becky and the Questmaster swapped roles, with him out-and-about and Becky producing in the studio. She also stood-in as the presenter of the *Treasure Quest: Extra Time* spin-off show that day.

Amy might only have worked on a few *Treasure Quest* programmes, but as the producer who was there right at the start she laid the foundations for everything that was to follow. And having experienced trying to solve her cryptic clues, the Questmaster claims that her riddles are far more devious and difficult than anything he could ever come up with!

R – *Radio Times*

For *Treasure Quest*'s two-part Easter specials, when Becky has to follow a double set of clues that take her across shows on both Easter Sunday and Easter Monday, the Questmaster always tries his best to push the boat out. Literally, in the case of the finale to the 2011 two-parter, which saw Becky having to don a pair of overalls and help out as an engineer on the Victorian steam launch *Falcon* at the Museum of the Broads in Stalham!

He's also sent Becky onto the rollercoaster at Great Yarmouth Pleasure Beach, into her encounters with the army at Swanton Morley and the fire service at North Earlham, had a clue hidden in a BBC Radio Norfolk programme from earlier in the week which listeners had to find online, and of course in 2010 sent Becky up for the second of her famous *Treasure Quest* helicopter trips.

The famous Becky Betts Radio Times cover from Easter 2010 in all its glory!

For the 2009 special, the Questmaster managed to arrange for one of the clues to be printed in the Easter Monday edition of the *Eastern Daily Press*. When trying to think of a way to top this the following year, he was struck by the idea that it would be nice to have a clue printed in the *Radio Times*, the BBC's famous radio and television listings magazine. (Other listings magazines are, of course, available).

Here there was a stroke of luck, as after contacting the magazine the Questmaster found that its Deputy Editor and Art Director, Shem Law, was familiar with the programme and indeed something of a fan! A plan was hatched that saw Becky Betts being interviewed for the magazine's 'Face Behind the Voice' section on its local radio listings pages, a feature which was printed in every edition of the Easter issue, bringing Becky to national attention! Secreted at the end of this feature, without Becky's knowledge, was a short clue prepared by the Questmaster, which would lead Becky to one of her destinations on Easter Monday.

But that wasn't where the *Radio Times* fun and games ended. As well as arranging for the interview and clue to be included in the magazine proper, Shem also prepared a custom-made, one-off copy of the Easter 2010 *Radio Times* which didn't feature *Doctor Who* on the cover as all the other copies did... but instead made a cover star out of BBC Radio Norfolk's very own Becky Betts!

The Questmaster arranged for this copy to be located at Victoria Stores in Mattishall, where Becky was led by one of her clues that Easter Monday morning, expecting only to be searching for a normal edition of the *Radio Times*. She screamed when she saw her own face looking out at her from the newsagent's magazine rack, and was all the more taken aback – not to mention rather crestfallen – when the Questmaster cruelly revealed that the entire interview with the *Radio Times* had been a set-up, designed purely to allow a clue to be included in the magazine. "They told me it was because so many people had written in!" she forlornly protested!

As for that particular copy of the *Radio Times* itself, it is now framed on the wall of her parents' kitchen in Suffolk. But Becky's *Treasure Quest* fame certainly spreads to that part of the world, and more than one visitor to the Betts household has been known to enquire on seeing it: "Excuse me, I have to ask... do you know Becky Betts?"

S – Stations

Railway stations have featured a great deal in *Treasure Quest*, and not just working ones either. Due to the Beeching Axe and other historical reasons, Norfolk is littered with buildings which were once busy and bustling railway stations for goods and passengers, but which are now empty and abandoned.

One such former station is located at Walpole Cross Keys, in West Norfolk very close to the border with Lincolnshire. Here the villagers have turned the long-abandoned site of the old railway station into the Eva Kemp Memorial Garden, with flowers now located along the lines of the old platforms. Becky found her treasure here one week in January 2010, hidden behind some old railway wheels that are affixed on display in the garden.

Not all old stations are simply left to disappear. Some are restored by heritage groups, such as Whitwell & Reepham Station. Becky found a clue there on a snowy day in November 2008, two months before the group looking after the station reopened it to the public for the first time in nearly fifty years. She later visited the station again when it was holding a steam rally. Becky has also found clues at stations which are

Becky hunts the platforms for a clue at Sheringham Station in October 2009.

now private houses, such as at Great Fransham or the old Royal Station at Wolferton.

Other railway stations across Norfolk are operated by groups such as the Bure Valley Railway, who look after Aylsham Station. Becky found her treasure at Aylsham in February 2009 during a 'Teddy Bear Express' event, when she had to go onto a train and find a person-sized teddy bear mascot guarding the treasure. Unfortunately, Becky hadn't anticipated that this bear would actually have a person inside it, so when she walked up to it in one of the carriages to claim the treasure, she was quite frightened when the bear stood up and moved!

Becky has also found clues with the North Norfolk Railway, the Barton House Railway, the Ashmanhaugh Light Railway and the Norton Hill Light Railway in Snettisham, among others. She's even had to actually take a ride on a mainline train on a memorable morning during the second day of the 2009 Easter two-parter, which she started in the village of Lingwood. Having been bamboozled by a clue hidden in that day's *Eastern Daily Press* newspaper, Becky was further confused when Navigator Ian – who was in cahoots with the Questmaster for this particular clue – took the radio car and left Becky marooned with her technical support, 'Engineer Steve'.

The listeners eventually realised the clue in the paper led Becky to catch a train at Lingwood station, and from looking at the satellite tracker online they could see that Ian was taking the radio car to Norwich to meet her at the other end. Utterly confused by the whole affair, Becky boarded the train, although she was somewhat reluctant to make a fool of herself by asking the guard if he had a clue for her. However, she found that he not only had the next clue on him, but also a travel pass to take her into Norwich!

After the short train journey from Lingwood into the city was completed, Becky and Steve were reunited with Ian and the car. However, she was quick to make him promise never to abandon her like that again!

T – Treasure

"To travel hopefully is a better thing than to arrive, and the true success is to labour." So claimed the Scottish writer Robert Louis Stevenson, in one of the essays included in his 1881 collection *Virginibus Puerisque, and Other Papers*. If BBC Radio Norfolk's *Treasure*

The special 100ᵗʰ Quest cake, Becky's treasure at the end of the 2010 Easter two-parter. It was made for the programme by a bakery in Drayton.

Quest were to adopt a programme motto then this quote would do quite nicely for it, pointing out as it does that the journey is more important than the destination. It is the fun and adventure Becky, David and the listeners have during a programme that are important and will be remembered, rather than whatever the Questmaster has seen fit to put inside the treasure envelope at the end of it.

Nonetheless, despite all of her *Treasure Quest* experience Becky doesn't quite seem to have learned not to have set her sights too high for the treasure, and is frequently heard to express disappointment if all she is rewarded with in a given week is a bit of paper with 'Treasure' written on it. In fairness to the Questmaster, however, it was not he who started the run of anti-climactic treasures. In the very first *Treasure Quest*, the Questmistress placed at the end of the trail an envelope which didn't even have anything as good as a bit of paper in it – it was, much to Becky's disbelief, completely empty!

Every now and then, though, the Questmaster does let Becky have something a little more interesting than a slip of paper or a sarcastic note. Occasionally the treasures have even been edible, and strangely these are the kind Becky has always appreciated the most! The most notable of these food-related rewards was the one Becky found at the end of her Easter *Treasure Quest* in April 2010. Perhaps mindful of the fact that she would have just gone through a helicopter journey she may not entirely have enjoyed, the Questmaster had commissioned a special cake to be placed at the treasure location, Dunston Hall.

As this epic Easter two-parter was, by coincidence, the one hundredth *Treasure Quest* on BBC Radio Norfolk, the large and impressive cake was shaped into the figures of the number '100'. Needless to say Becky was quick to tuck in, but there was plenty left over to be shared out back at the BBC Radio Norfolk offices. *Treasure Quest*'s regular sports bulletin reader Richard Hancock is believed to have eventually claimed the biggest share!

Often the reason the treasures are, frankly, nothing much to write home about is because the Questmaster has a particular rule about them. He doesn't believe licence fee payers' money should be spent on providing frivolous gifts to Becky Betts, so he pays for them out of his own pocket – which is why they very rarely end up being anything that costs any money at all!

U – Underground

Radio programmes, especially live ones, only rarely venture underneath the ground. This is for the very good and practical reason that it's much more difficult to actually get a signal from any piece of equipment when you're beneath the earth rather than above it or somewhere high up! This has not, however, stopped *Treasure Quest* from giving it a go on various occasions, although Becky's adventures under the ground have often resulted in some of what David likes to refer to as the show's "dark side of the moon" moments when, like the American Apollo spacecraft when they travelled behind the moon, communication with Becky is impossible until she reappears out of the darkness.

Becky first disappeared off down below for *Treasure Quest* purposes in June 2008, when she found a clue in the lime kiln at Litcham's small museum. This was a particularly fraught and difficult *Treasure Quest* morning and losing communication with Becky when she went down to the kiln was the least of the programme's problems. Before she had even managed to find it, Becky and the listeners had misinterpreted part of the clue and thought she actually had to go to the cellars of Litcham's pub, The Bull.

As this was quite early on in the show's run, and not as many people in Norfolk were familiar with what *Treasure Quest* was and how it worked as they would later be, the landlord of The Bull, confronted with Becky Betts having turned up on his doorstep out of the blue, wasn't quite sure what was going on. So, when Becky asked him whether he had a clue for BBC Radio Norfolk's *Treasure Quest*, he did what any polite and helpful soul would have done in the situation – he said "I'm sure we can find something, yes."

So Becky ended up being led all around the pub, exploring all of its nooks and crannies and indeed cellars, to no avail. In desperation she eventually implored the landlord to tell her whether he had a clue, and he confessed that he did not. "Then where can we find an old lime kiln?" she asked, frantically. "A lime kiln?" he replied. "We haven't got one of those. You want the museum for that..."

Another of Becky's underground exploits was actually captured on video in November 2009, when she was being filmed for the behind-the-scenes video to be shown at that year's *Treasure Quest Live!* event. The final clue took her to the cellars of Byford's in Holt, where Becky went down to where the treasure envelope was, stood mere feet away from it, but couldn't see it. She claimed that all the time she was out of communication with the studio she was frantically running around trying to find the treasure, and was horrified when all of the shots that made it into the finished video showed her casually wandering about, looking really quite sedate!

Becky is by no means the only *Treasure Quest* 'runner' to have been sent underground, however. In June 2010 Kirsteen Thorne had to retrieve a clue from some historic tunnels underneath a shop called Adcock's in Watton. The real history was unveiled after she had found the clue and come back above ground, though, when the owner of the shop produced an old black-and-white photograph of the premises being opened by celebrity guest David Clayton back in the 1980s!

V – VC Norwich

VC Norwich stands for 'Velo Club' Norwich – a local cycling group which often starts its Sunday morning rides from outside The Forum in Norwich, the big glass-and-steel building just off the marketplace, which among other uses houses the studios of BBC Radio Norfolk and BBC *Look East*. One of the members of VC Norwich is freelance journalist Bob Carter, who can often be found working shifts on the BBC Radio Norfolk news and sports desks.

A keen cyclist, Bob had recently cycled the route of the Norfolk leg of the Tour of Britain for a BBC Radio Norfolk feature. He came up with the idea that it would be fun to put Becky onto a bicycle one week, and approached the

Kirsteen chats to BBC Radio Norfolk's Paul Hayes after her Treasure Quest bike ride in September 2010.

Questmaster about arranging it. Everything was set up for Becky to have a short cycle ride across Norwich one morning in September 2010, to take her from her starting point to her second clue, which would be located with the VC Norwich members gathering outside of The Forum. However, in the event Becky managed to escape from the bike ride without knowing it, as she fell ill that weekend and her regular substitute Kirsteen Thorne had to step in. Nonetheless, the bike ride went ahead, even though Kirsteen confessed once the bikes were revealed that she hadn't been on one for quite some time! She went on to prove that the old adage is true, however – that once you've learned how, you never forget!

Even though Becky missed out on the bike ride, she has been put onto various other forms of transport during her *Treasure Quest* adventures over the years. She's had to have a go at riding on 'Penny Pony', one of the animals kept at Aylsham Fun Barns; she's travelled in style in a vintage steam car that took her down to the famous steam rally at Strumpshaw; and she's clambered up into a fair few tractors in her time at various ploughing matches and machinery days.

She's had to make her way across water on more than one occasion, such as when she and Ian had to paddle their way to the centre of the boating lake at Cromer, to retrieve a treasure fixed to a buoy in the middle. She's also had to make her way across the River Yare on the Reedham Ferry on a couple of occasions, including one in June 2008 when a clue was located on the actual chain ferry itself.

W – Weather

The Questmaster likes to think that he can control pretty much everything that goes on during *Treasure Quest*, although that's always something of a misguided notion when you're producing a programme which is centred around the whirlwind that is Becky Betts.

One element the Questmaster certainly cannot exert any influence over is the weather. This is why when Becky's helicopter flights have been sprung upon her, the Questmaster has always had his fingers tightly crossed hoping for clear skies so that the take-offs could go ahead. Fortunately the weather was kind on both of those occasions – but it's not always so generous!

Warm weather rarely causes *Treasure Quest* any problems, apart from when Becky is left in a fragile condition after too much time out in the sun, and starts to complain about her "tomato" appearance! It's the cold that really starts to cause the programme issues – particularly for the radio car duo, who have more than once been heard to point out that the heating in the radio car is not all that it could be!

Snow and ice provide the worst conditions for *Treasure Quest* to face, as the safety of the radio car team is always the primary concern. As much as we always want to see Becky and Ian out and about solving

The radio car in the snow at Besthorpe, in January 2010.

the clues, we would never want them risking life and limb purely for the sake of a radio entertainment show.

That's why *Treasure Quest* had its first ever abandonment in November 2008. When Norfolk was being lashed by heavy snow, conditions got progressively worse one morning. Things didn't get off to the best of starts when the radio car mast froze in its upward position early in the morning, at Taverham. With the mast frozen up, the car couldn't be moved and, all the worse for Becky that particular morning, the heating couldn't be turned on!

Eventually, with the aid of generous quantities of anti-freeze, Ian was able to get the mast down, but the snow got worse and worse. Having battled two hours into the programme and found clue four at Chaucher House in Bawdeswell, it decided that enough was enough. The show was declared a draw, Becky and Ian went no further, and instead very slowly made their way back to base in Norwich. "You know what this means, don't you?" Becky asked. "We can go sledging!"

At least on that occasion they actually made it out, and most of the way around. The weekend before Christmas in December 2010, the snow – and more importantly, the ice – was judged to be so bad that late on Saturday evening David Clayton took the decision that it was too risky to send the radio car out on Sunday. This was the first ever non-start in *Treasure Quest*'s history – and so far, the only one. However, Becky rather enjoyed being in the studio with David, playing best-of clips and highlights from *Treasure Quest Live!*, especially as it meant she was able to sit in the warm and enjoy a fast food breakfast!

X – X1 bus

The X1 bus route is reputed by some to be the longest in the country. Every day the service winds its way from Lowestoft to Peterborough and, of course, back the other way, stopping off at Great Yarmouth, Norwich, King's Lynn and various points in between. It's difficult to know whether such a nebulous thing as a bus route can be said to have attained cult status. But if any bus route can claim it, then the X1 would certainly be at the front of the queue – it even has a blog, with over a thousand entries so far, dedicated to it. 'The X1 Blog' is written by Gerard Fletcher from Walpole St Peter, who has even seen his website about the comings and goings of the service featured in *The Sun*.

The X1 bus which Becky had to catch for a clue – much to her discomfort!

It was at Hockering, one of the smaller destinations along the X1's 120-odd mile route, that Becky Betts encountered one of the buses on Easter Monday 2010. The Questmaster had arranged for a clue to be located with a passenger 'planted' on the bus – a broad Norfolk cleaning lady character called 'Mrs H', played by friend of the radio station Jenny Harmer – with Becky having to actually get on the bus, travel on it to the next stop with Ian following behind in the radio car, and get the clue from Mrs H.

Unfortunately, given that this was the X1 coming from Peterborough rather than the one going to it, a lot of the passengers were not familiar with BBC Radio Norfolk or *Treasure Quest* and had absolutely no idea as to what this mad woman from the BBC was doing there! This made Becky rather timid about asking anybody whether they had the clue, so Mrs H ended up having to practically bully her off the bus at the correct stop to give her the envelope.

This is by no means the only time Becky has needed to find a bus to get a clue, however, or even the only time she has had to travel on one for the programme. Having heard Becky's unease at her bus journey in the Easter special, Richard Dixon from the Eastern Transport Collection Society wrote to the Questmaster offering a ride in one of their historic buses later that April. They would be running trips along the North Norfolk coast for an event at Sheringham station on Sunday the 18th, and perhaps the Questmaster might like to send Becky aboard one of their vehicles?

The Questmaster, of course, leapt at the chance, and so on that Sunday Becky Betts found herself bounding up to the top deck of a 1954 Bristol LD double-decker with Eastern CoachWorks body from

Becky takes a ride aboard a more classic vehicle, from Cromer to Sheringham in April 2010.

Lowestoft. After issuing a ticket from a vintage Setright machine, Becky enjoyed a rather more relaxed journey than her X1 adventure, travelling in style from Cromer to Sheringham, leaving David Clayton green with envy back in the studio. David is something of a bus obsessive, having become enamoured of them during his journeys to school aboard them in the 1960s, and would have dearly loved to have been in Becky's place on that particular morning!

Y – You

The listeners are the people without whom the show couldn't happen – and that means you! It would be a very dull programme, and Becky would never get anywhere, if we didn't have all of you calling, texting, e-mailing, Facebooking and occasionally even Tweeting in each and every week with your suggestions for how to solve the cryptic riddles and where Becky should head next.

But it's not just solving the clues – our listeners have gone to all sorts of extraordinary lengths to show their support for the programme. Whether it's sending in money in the programme's name for Children in Need, making signs to hold up by the side of the road to encourage Becky as the radio car goes past, or even excitedly heading to the clue location to meet Becky and Ian if they've realised the radio car is coming to somewhere in their own town or village!

It was also a listener who set up the very popular *Treasure Quest* Facebook group, where fans discuss and debate the clues, and sometimes even post their own photos of Becky out and about during the course of the morning, before the pictures Navigator Ian takes each week are put there the day after the Quest. Many listeners have also thronged to *Treasure Quest* events such as the live shows at the Norwich Playhouse and the calendar signing at The Forum, and have even sent the station gifts and cards for Becky and the team at Christmas, or occasionally at other random times through the year. One listener sent Becky a special 'Suffolk Passport' for her occasional *Treasure Quest* trips across the border, including with it an 'emergency ration' of a slice of toast! A number of you have also suggested clue locations to the Questmaster and volunteered to be clue holders putting the envelopes in place on the day, getting the chance to meet Becky and become a part of the programme.

Treasure Quest has gained so many listeners that it has become the most popular show broadcast on Sundays on any radio station in Norfolk – including the national ones! And even though the bulk of

our audience obviously listens in the county, that isn't the only place where the show has avid fans. As well as people in the neighbouring counties listening on our radio frequencies, *Treasure Quest* has, down the years, attracted e-mails and Facebook messages from online listeners in places such as Manchester,

One of the many gifts sent in by listeners down the years – in this case, a custom-made Treasure Quest clock!

Glasgow, Dublin, Norway, Switzerland, Sweden, Croatia, Lanzarote, Austria, Canada, the United States and South Africa!

Z – Zoos

Becky has twice visited zoos in Norfolk during the course of her *Treasure Quest* travels. The first of these visits was in June 2009, although she didn't actually have to deal with any animal life on that particular occasion, as her clue was located in the café of the Amazona Zoo at Cromer. She made up for that, though, on her second zoo visit, which came at Banham Zoo in South Norfolk in November 2010.

The week she went to Banham saw Becky run out of time to find the treasure, although as she was close to it the Questmaster still allowed her to go on after the news and speak to Nick Conrad during his programme. At the zoo Becky was led to the brand new snow leopard cubs, whose enclosure had been the location of the treasure envelope – although safely on the outside, of course, rather than Becky having had to go in with the leopards to retrieve it!

One of Becky's most memorable animal encounters came not at a zoo as such, but at an aquatic equivalent – the Sea Life Centre in Great Yarmouth, where she found her treasure for a show in October 2009. As occasionally happens, Becky had a task to undertake before she was allowed to have the treasure envelope – on this occasion, she

Becky has a go at feeding the sharks at the Sea Life Centre in Great Yarmouth, October 2009.

had to try her hand at 'target feeding' the centre's nurse sharks, an activity designed to help stop the creatures from becoming bored.

Becky was rather unsettled by the sharks – one of whom was rather incongruously named 'Nigel' – and squealed at the way in which they "sucked in" the food she had to drop into the tank for them. Her squeals of "I don't like it!" may have frightened the sharks more than she was frightened of them, although Navigator Ian seemed to get along rather better with the creatures!

Sharks aren't the only animal Becky turns out to be frightened of, with various phobias having come to the fore during her *Treasure Quest* duties. When finding a clue at Blacksmith's Cottage Nursery – home of BBC Radio Norfolk Saturday gardener Ben Potterton – in November 2008, Becky had to take refuge behind Ben when she revealed that she was terrified of his horde of advancing... turkeys!

Alpacas have also been shown to rather unsettle the Becky Betts constitution. Perhaps surprisingly, Norfolk has at least two alpaca farms, which *Treasure Quest* has visited. The alpaca farm at Letton, between Dereham and Watton, was a clue location in December 2009, but Becky didn't like the herds of alpacas all around her in the barn there, and had to get Navigator Ian to go closer in to grab the clue. She was even more frightened in April 2011 when visiting Alpacas of East Anglia at Beighton, near Acle, claiming that the alpacas there were following her! "It's because they're so tall," she explained of her fear of the placid creatures. "They look as if they're about to headbutt you..."

Given this alpaca-phobia, Becky was less than impressed at the second *Treasure Quest Live!* stage show in November 2010 when, as one of the 'Guess the Guest' rounds for the matinee performance, she had to don a blindfold and try and identify a guest which turned out to be... a stuffed alpaca! She needed some reassurance that it wasn't a living creature, despite its complete lack of sound, smell or movement!

The alpacas keep a watchful eye on Becky at Beighton, near Acle, on Easter Monday 2011.

While on her Treasure Quest travels in October 2009, Becky comes across a battered copy of an old BBC Radio Norfolk book with a familiar-seeming co-writer!

Another accolade for the office wall! This is the Silver Award which Treasure Quest won in the 'Interactivity' category at the 2009 Frank Gillard Awards. The awards are given annually, to recognise achievements by the BBC's local radio stations.

Afterword

By Greg James
Presenter, BBC Radio 1

I've never written an afterword before. Or a foreword, for that matter. This is very exciting. Does anyone read an afterword? I don't think I'd be reading this as it's such an achievement to finish a book that when it's done, it's done. What more could I possibly add?

Oh well, I'll give it a go.

I do feel slightly fraudulent writing this, actually. Not only because I've not had anything to do with the creation or execution of *Treasure Quest*, but because I was never really properly employed by BBC Radio Norfolk. Now, if that sentence didn't stop you reading then I don't know what will! Are you still with me? Good – then I'll continue.

My relationship with BBC Radio Norfolk is a funny one. It was 2004. I was a keen, annoying and lanky student from the UEA and I pestered Jim Cassidy to let me 'come in and make the tea'. This seems to be the 'thing' to do. Although I don't really remember making much tea. Except for Bumfrey – he was a slave-driver.

From that initial chat with Jim, I was kind of 'in'. It was a really wonderful place to learn about this thing I was fascinated with – *radio*. It's been my life since I caught the bug when I was ten. It's all I've wanted to work in and BBC Radio Norfolk helped me so much. I was a regular nervous 'sofa guest' on Stephen Bumfrey's Breakfast Show, where I fumbled my way through the newspapers; I helped out at a couple of the Royal Norfolk Shows; and I was around most Saturdays to help out and watch a master at work on *Saturday Sport*. The master of course being Matthew Gudgin. I was and still am in awe of how he does that show. One of my favourite broadcasters – it's so effortless. He and Stephen in particular are great inspirations to me because they do radio properly.

In fact, BBC Radio Norfolk does radio properly. All the presenters do. That is why it is so loved and that's why I love it. It's proper radio *for the listeners*. That might sound like a strange statement but there is so much radio that I listen to that isn't really *for* anyone. Stupid people sometimes forget that they are there to entertain, engage with and relate to the listeners in whatever way they think is right. If radio starts sounding like a 'party you're not invited to', you'll go home – or go to another party. BBC Radio Norfolk is never the party you're not invited to. Everyone is welcome and everyone *feels* welcome. Even as an 18-year-old nobody who wasn't even from 'these parts', I was made to feel welcome – and I still feel the same.

Feeling 'part of it' is one of the many reasons for *Treasure Quest*'s huge success. The listeners love it because it involves *them*. And it is, like all the great radio ideas, totally silly. I base my whole show around the motto 'it has to be about the listeners and it *has* to be stupid and silly'. There are many moments of greatness talked about in this book, including the bit that I featured (and still regularly feature) on my show where Becky was stuck in a helicopter shouting at David *and* the pilot. The famous catchphrase "David I am gonna throttle you!" was born.

Treasure Quest is a true 'Oh why didn't *I* think of that?' radio idea. These are the best. It's been copied and adapted many times over by several different stations, which is testament enough to its success. In fact, that's given me an idea…

How about a BBC Radio 1 *Treasure Quest*? I'd love to get Fearne Cotton into a helicopter…

Greg James
September 2011

Becky Betts, ready for anything at the start of another Quest, in October 2010. Through rain, wind, hail, snow, clues on village signs, being repeatedly unable to say the word 'Massachusetts', radio car breakdowns and yet more clues on village signs, Becky and the team continue to do their best to inform, educate and above all entertain you on a Sunday morning.

Thank you for reading, and thank you for listening.

About the author
Paul Hayes joined BBC Radio Norfolk full-time in March 2008, where he has worked on a variety of programmes as a producer and as a presenter. He started at the station as a one-day-a-week volunteer phone answerer in August 2006, in an attempt to escape a career pushing paper around local government offices. Having been born and raised in West Sussex, he arrived in Norfolk in 2002 to study English Literature at the University of East Anglia. He lives in a small flat in Norwich with a pot plant which never flowers.

Acknowledgements
For their help and support in the writing of this book I would like to thank all of the *Treasure Quest* family at BBC Radio Norfolk, past and present, particularly David Clayton, Becky Betts, Ian Forster and Alexajain Wills-Bradfield.

Special thanks to Elsje Stocker, whose tenacity and practicality turned this book from a theoretical exercise into an actual product, and without whose hard work it would not have been possible. I am also deeply grateful to Norman Macintosh and all at Charity Goods, whose efforts have not only made this book a reality but also raised many thousands of pounds for Children in Need through a plethora of products down the years.

Thanks are also due to Martyn Weston, Graham Barnard, Tim Sparrow, Emma Philpotts, Rob Sykes, Ben Debuse, Peter Waters, Chris Garrod, Tim Pieraccini, Richard Walker, Joanne Brown, Stewart Milner, Neil Collins, Bill Richmond, Alison Smith, Simon Ellard, Lara Parkin, Greg James and Ben Robertson.

Last but by no means least, thank you to everyone who has ever been a *Treasure Quest* clue holder, and to all of the *Treasure Quest* listeners. Several of you had suggested to us down the years that we should do a book – we hope that you have enjoyed the end result!